KESARIYA

Born and brought up in Marwar, **Urvashi Singh** is the twentieth-generation descendant of Rao Karamsiji, the fifteenth-century founder of Kheenvsar (Khimsar). She received her education at Mayo College Girls' School, Ajmer. A Political Science graduate from Lady Shri Ram College (LSR), University of Delhi, Urvashi went on to complete her Master's in Gender, Media and Culture at the London School of Economics and Political Science.

She founded her publication, *Rajputana Collective,* in 2017 and currently runs her own resort in the Himalayas. A photographer, entrepreneur and autoimmune philanthropist, she resides in Manali with her homegrown community, a motorcycle and three mischievous yet adorable dogs.

'This book will prove to be an important milestone in the preservation and dissemination of our rich cultural heritage and historical legacy.'

—Jagdeep Dhankar
Former Vice President of India

'The Rajput dynasties of Rajasthan not only protected the motherland but also made invaluable contributions to art, culture and architecture. This book aptly captures their indomitable spirit and timeless legacy.'

—Bhajan Lal Sharma
Chief Minister of Rajasthan

'It is a matter of joy that the glorious history of the Karamsot Rathores is being researched, compiled and published in the form of a history book.'

—Diya Kumari
Deputy Chief Minister of Rajasthan

'I appreciate this effort to make the history of the Karamsot Rathores accessible to readers. It will serve as an important reference point for generations to come.'

—Col. Rajyavardhan Singh Rathore
Minister of Youth Affairs and Sports,
Government of Rajasthan

'I am delighted to learn of the publication of this book. It will serve as an inspiration for generations of Rajputs to come.'

—Gajendra Singh Shekhawat
Union Minister of Culture and Tourism,
Government of India

'My son, Dhananjai, and daughter, Urvashi Singh, have contributed wholeheartedly to the writing and publication of this book. I give my blessings to both of them. This book stands as a testament to their dedication and love for our family's heritage.'

—Raja Gajendra Singh Khimsar

'I hope to have the opportunity to read and learn about the sacrifices of the Karamsot Rathores in this book, and trust that the younger generation will imbibe their values and contribute to the progress of our country.'

—Rajendra Singh Rathore
Former Minister, Government of Rajasthan

'I hope this book inspires both present and future generations.'

—Rao Rajendra Singhji
Member of Parliament

'Through this book, our brave ancestors are being commemorated. The inspiring tales of their valour and sacrifice shall reach present and future generations alike.'

—Arun Singh
Member of Parliament

'History illuminates the story of human success and gives humankind an opportunity to feel proud and inspired by its legacy. History also teaches valuable lessons and guides one towards a brighter future. This book embodies those very ideals, preserving the inspiring saga of the Karamsot Rathores for generations to come.'

—Kunwar Dhananjai Singh Khimsar

'The history of a man's ancestors is the measure of his present actions. This work stands as a fitting tribute to the courage and legacy of the Karamsot Rathores.'

—Lakshman Singh
Chief of the Shree Kshatriya Yuvak Sangh

KESARIYA

AN ODE TO THE KARAMSOT RATHORES OF KHEENVSAR

URVASHI SINGH

RUPA

Published by
Rupa Publications India Pvt. Ltd 2025
161-B/4, Gulmohar House,
Yusuf Sarai Community Centre,
New Delhi 110049

Sales centres:
Bengaluru Chennai
Hyderabad Kolkata Mumbai

P-ISBN: 978-93-7003-259-0
E-ISBN: 978-93-7003-773-1

First impression 2025

10 9 8 7 6 5 4 3 2 1

Printed in India

To my mother
Rani Priti Kumari Singh

You went too soon,
but I shall forever carry you in my heart.

Contents

Let me tell you what I wish I'd known
When I was young and dreamed of glory
You have no control

Who lives
Who dies
Who tells your story?

[…]

But when you're gone, who remembers your name?
Who keeps your flame?
Who tells your story?
Who tells your story?
Who tells your story?

[…]

Time.

—*Hamilton* by Lin-Manuel Miranda

Author's Note

1. Many historical archives mention chronology as per the lunisolar Hindu calendar or Vikrami calendar, which mentions years in the Vikram Samvat (V.S.) format. Vikram Samvat is generally 57 years ahead of the Christian Era, which follows the Gregorian Calendar. In present times, most of the contemporary world uses the solar dating system of the Gregorian calendar, so I have used all chronological references in accordance with it. I write all years followed by CE (Common Era), a more secular equivalent of AD (Anno Domini), the Latin phrase meaning 'in the year of the Lord'.

   However, given that the common lunar and solar sidereal years of the Vikram Samvat do not necessarily correspond with 12 months, a correctional leap month is added (adhik maas) or subtracted (khyaat maas) as per the Metonic cycle, which falls once every three years. A more precise calculation indicates a lag of 56.7 years in the Gregorian calendar compared to the Vikram Samvat. For scholarly convenience, this book uses a standard formula of 57 years. For example, 1348 V.S. = 1291 CE (1348 minus 57).

   Rounding up 56.7 by an additional 0.3 is sure to cause some conversional discrepancies, but I use this chronological yardstick as per standard historiographical norms. For a closer correlation of the actual date, I encourage my readers to refer to the sources mentioned at the end of the book, using which they can verify the timelines on which my work relies. I would also like to specify that all chronology mentioned in the book is in complete accordance with Dr Mahendra Singh Tanwar's Hindi manuscript. The incidence of any factual discrepancies, therefore, must be pardoned. I encourage my discerning readers to refer to his research volume, which was originally published in Hindi.

2. I mention several Hindi and Marwari words in italics upon their first mention as prompts for the reader to seek in the book's glossary.
3. All additional notes, references and bibliographical citations are mentioned in the endnotes. As the author, I do not lay claim to any external sources and have used them solely for reference. Many bibliographical citations have been adapted from Dr Mahendra Tanwar's Hindi manuscript, and because a majority of this book is a translation of his scholarly achievement, my work entirely relies on the facts and citations stated in his book.

Foreword

I am delighted to see that after so many years of hard work and deliberation, the book on Karamsots is getting published. In the history of this Rathore clan of Marwar, the Karamsot Rathores have been gallant heroes and have immensely contributed to Marwar's history. Rao Jodhaji was the famous founder of the city of Jodhpur, who descended from Rao Sihaji, the father of the Rathores of Marwar. His equally worthy son, Rao Karamsiji, guided by the light of his ancestors, with valour and bravery, took the Rathore territory further and established himself in Kheenvsar. With the passing of time, this branch of Rathores came to be known as the Karamsot Rathores, and they eventually disseminated to different parts of Marwar. Kheenvsar is one of the most well-established forts of Marwar and is the main seat of the Karamsot Rathores.

The most important and relevant part of history is the tales of princes and the valour of one's own clan. It should be our utmost endeavour to conserve the historical heritage of our ancestors and present it to the future generations. I am glad that Raja Gajendra Singh of Kheenvsar has been able to compile the glorious history of his clan and commissioned Dr Mahendra Singh Tanwar to write and publish the Hindi volume. The dream of his beloved grandfather Thakur Kesri Singhji is finally coming true. Thakur Sahab was a knowledgeable person, and he took a major interest in preserving the history of his ancestors. Taking this legacy forward, Raja Onkar Singhji also preserved these valuable stories and often narrated them to me. Kumari Urvashi has also played a valuable role in this project by providing an English translation of the writing in accordance with the wishes of Raja Gajendra Singh.

My compliments to Dr Mahendra Singh Tanwar for this scholarly presentation, and I pray to Maa Nagana Mata to give him the knowledge to continue to propagate the glory of Rathore history in all his future endeavours.

—Maharaja Gaj Singhji II
Marwar–Jodhpur

Introduction

India's glorious histories are interwoven with the timeless heroic sagas of its warrior scions, the Kshatriyas. The ever-inspiring traditions of virtue, sacrifice and loyalty run deep within the Kshatriya veins and infuse every forthcoming generation with their unique resplendence. Endless inheritors have smeared their valiant Kshatriya legacy on gleaming swords and bled tears, sweat and blood to reap their motherlands.

Amongst the Suryavanshi branch of Kshatriyas, one clan of Rajputs is believed to have originated from Lord Indra's *ratha* or spine.[1] The Rashtrakutas, as this dynasty was popularly known, had ruled over Kannauj for several generations before one of its princes, Rao Sihaji, shifted his locus westwards. In the late 13th century, Rao Siha conquered Pali to establish the bravest dynasty that would nurture the arid desert sands of Marwar. Thus, the Rathore dynasty was born.

Every breeze that gushes past the ombré folds of the Thar reverberates Rathori greatness and the distinct embellishments of conquests that they brought to their land. Rao Jodha, the 15th Rathore ruler, carried his ancestral surge into the west by founding a new empire that would be named after him as Jodhpur or the land of Rao Jodha. He gave rise to a powerful appendage of sons, each of whom unfurled the Rathore flag in various expansions of their father's kingdom, thereby fortifying their dynastic stronghold in the region. While Rao Bika, the second son of Rao Jodha, established his dynasty in Bikaner, his younger brother, Rao Duda, did the same in Merta. Rao Karamsiji, the eighth son of Jodhpur, laid his sovereign foundation in Kheenvsar in 1823. Ever since its iconic founding ruler, Kheenvsar has nurtured 21 generations of Karamsot Rathores.

The Karamsot Rathores would thereafter establish their strongholds over the lands of Bikaner, Kishangarh and several other *sirayats.*[2] Many of them have sacrificed their lives fighting for the glory of Marwar and defending its people against invaders.

Meanwhile, the contemporary generations of Rao Karamsiji have made noteworthy contributions to politics and development in post-independence India. Raja Gajendra Singh of Kheenvsar, the 19th direct descendant of Rao Karamsiji, consolidated his role as the custodian of his familial legacy not just in the form of an illustrious career but also by commissioning the supreme task of Karamsot historiography in the form of *Karamsot Rathoron ka Gauraveeya Itihaas.* It is due to his unending support and guidance that I have successfully compiled the extensive history of such a gallant clan.

When I commenced my role as the chief executor of this onerous anthology in 2012, I assumed my research to focus on not more than 25–30 villages. However, as I proceeded to explore the myriad veneers of Karamsot historiography, I found that the strength of these villages exceeded over 100. My meticulous work on illustrating Rao Karamsiji's clan has spanned over eight enriching years, and I have reached a point in my experiential journey where I have grown deeply attached to these glorious annals.

Even though there hasn't been a single day that my passionate attention as a researcher has flickered, I ask for your forgiveness should you find any shortcomings on my part. As a historian would know best, history never attains completion and is an ever-flowing stream of actions, events and experiences. Moreover, mine is but an initial excavation into the magnificent reserves of historical wealth that lie buried in the vast chasms of Marwar. It is my sincere endeavour to spark the curiosity of many subsequent researchers and inspire supplementary efforts that will take forth the task of documenting the living history of Karamsot Rathores as well as their future destinies. It takes but little time for the future to unfold into the present, before it is swiftly consigned to the past.

To write history is a complex piece of art, and the lack of potential content often compels a historian to rely on derelict, albeit available, material. That withstanding, I have conveyed my role as the prime historiographer of the Karamsot Rathores without discrimination and with utmost transparency.

To pursue comprehensive historical research, I have relied on diverse records and sources, without which these historical volumes could not have been possible. While it is not feasible for me to mention the extensive list of creditors, I will mention some primary records and sources that have been fundamental to my research. These include official archives from Kheenvsar, Bikaner, Rajasthan State Archives as well as the National Archives of India. The Maharaja Man Singh Pustak Prakash Research Centre, the Mehrangarh Museum Trust, the Rajasthan Oriental Research Institute, Rajasthani Shodh

Sansthan (Chopasni) as well as the many historical records and manuscripts stored across various research organizations have been crucial contributors to my work. The accounts of various living Karamsots, from the elderly to their younger offshoots, have exhilarated my work by providing their candid and heartfelt accounts that have added heavily towards the inclusivity of these volumes.

Last, but certainly not least, I extend my sincere gratitude to H.H. Maharaja Gaj Singhji of Jodhpur for digitizing the extensive archives of Marwar and making them available online. Without this generous initiative, it would have been impossible for a humble historian to access and study over 5,000 scattered archival records.

I thank all those I have enlisted as well as those I will mention in the near future. Your patience, support and belief are integral to the history you are about to uncover.

—Dr Mahendra Singh Tanwar
1 December 2020
Jodhpur

Timeline

YEAR	RULE	CENTRE	MARWAR		KHEENVSAR	NOTES
1200	**SLAVE DYNASTY** (1200–1273)					
1206		**SLAVE DYNASTY** (Qutbuddin Aibak)				
1210		Aram Shah				
1211		Iltutmish				
1236		Razia Sultan				
1250			1. Rao Sihaji (1250–1273)			
1266		Ghiyasuddin Balban (1266–1273)				
1273				2. Rao Asthanji (1273–1292)		
1288	**KHALJIS** (1288–1312)	Muizuddin Qaiqabad				
1290		**KHALJIS** Jalaluddin (Firuz) Khalji (1290–1292)				
1292			3. Rao Dhuhadji (1292–1309)			
1296		Alauddin Khalji (1296–1312)				
1309				4. Rao Raipalji (1309–1313)		
1313			5. Rao Kanpalji (1313–1323)			

YEAR	RULE	CENTRE	MARWAR		KHEENVSAR	NOTES
1317	**TUGHLAQS** (1317–1374)	Qutbuddin Mubarak Shah Khalji murdered by Khusrau Khan				
1320		**TUGHLAQS** Ghiyathaldin Tughlaq (1320–1323) killed by Muhammad bin Tughlaq				
1323				6. Rao Jalansiji (1323–1328)		
1326		Muhammad bin Tughlaq (1326–1344)				
1328			7. Rao Chadaji (1328–1344)			
1344				8. Rao Teedaji (1344–1357)		
1352		Feroz Shah Tughlaq (1352–1374)				
1357			9. Rao Salkhaji (1357–1374)			
1370				10. Rao Veeramji (1370–1383)		
1389		Strife				
1394		**SULTAN DYNASTY** Nasiruddin Mahmud Shah vs Nasiruddin Nusrat Shah	11. Rao Chundaji (1394–1423)			
1398		**TIMUR'S LOOT**				
1415	**SAYYIDS** (1415–1427)	**SAYYID DYNASTY** (1415–1427)				

YEAR	RULE	CENTRE	MARWAR		KHEENVSAR	NOTES
1423				12. Rao Kanaji (1423–1424)		
1424			13. Rao Sataji (1424–1427)			
1427				14. Rao Ridmalji (1427–1438)		
1451	**LODIS** (1451–1517)	**LODI DYNASTY** Bahlul Khan Lodi (1451–1467)				
1453			**15. Rao Jodhaji** (1453–1489)			
1467					1. Rao Karamsiji departed from Jodhpur to establish his stronghold in Nadsar, Aasop (1467–1492)	
1489		Sikandar Lodi (Nizam Khan) (1489–1515)		16. Rao Satalji (1489–1492)		
1492			17. Rao Sujaji (1492–1515)			
1494					**Rao Karamsiji establishes Kheenvsar**	
1515				18. Rao Gangaji (1515–1532)		
1517		Ibrahim Khan Lodi				

YEAR	RULE	CENTRE	MARWAR		KHEENVSAR	NOTES
1526		**BATTLE OF PANIPAT**			Rao Karamsiji is martyred on 28 June 1526 while fighting a battle in Narnaul	
1527	**MUGHALS** (1527–1532)	**MUGHALS** Babur			2. Rao Pichyaansiji (1527–1540)	
1530		Humayun (1530–1532)				
1532			19. Rao Maldeo (1532–1562)			
1540		Sher Shah Suri and Islam Shah Suri (1540–1544)				
1544	**MUGHALS** (1544–1843)				3. Rao Maheshdasji (1544–1556)	
1555		Humayun				
1556		Akbar (1556–1593)				
1562				20. Rao Chandrasen (1562–1581)	4. Rao Hardasji (1562–1605)	
1582			21. Rao Rai Singhji (1582–1583)			
1583				22. Mota Raja Udai Singhji (1583–1595)		
1589						Kheenvsar is made into a satellite state under Jodhpur

YEAR	RULE	CENTRE	MARWAR		KHEENVSAR	NOTES
1595			23. Sawai Raja Sur Singhji (1595–1619)			
1605		Jahangir (1605–1619)				
1617					5. Thakur Dayaldasji (1617–1643)	
1619				24. Maharaja Gaj Singhji I (1619–1638)		
1627		Shah Jahan I (1627–1643)				
1638			25. Maharaja Jaswant Singhji I (1638–1678)			
1658		Aurangzeb (1658–1670)			6. Thakur Bhim Singhji	
1670					7. Thakur Harnath Singhji (1670–1707)	
1707		Bahadur Shah I (Shah Alam I)		26. Maharaja Ajit Singhji (1707–1724)		
1708					8. Thakur Udai Singhji (1708–1729)	
1712		Jahandar Shah				
1713		Farrukhsiyar				

YEAR	RULE	CENTRE	MARWAR		KHEENVSAR	NOTES
1719		Shah Jahan II				
1720		Muhammad Shah (1720–1730)				
1724			27. Maharaja Abhay Singhji (1724–1749)			
1730					9. Thakur Zorawar Singhji (1730–1772)	
1748		Ahmad Shah Bahadur (1748–1752)				
1749				28. Maharaja Ram Singhji (1749–1751)		
1751			29. Maharaja Bakhat Singhji (1751–1752)			
1752				30. Maharaja Vijay Singhji (1752–1793)		
1753		Alamgir II				
1759		Shah Jahan III				
1760		Shah Alam II (1760–1803)				
1772					10. Thakur Karan Singhji (1772–1782)	

YEAR	RULE	CENTRE	MARWAR		KHEENVSAR	NOTES
1782					11. Thakur Berisal Singhji (1782–1786)	
1790					*Thakur Bhom Singhji Zorawarsinghot* (1790–1793)	
1793			31. Maharaja Bhim Singhji (1793–1803)			
1796					*Thakur Pratap Singhji Bhomsinghot* (1796–1808)	
1803				32. Maharaja Man Singhji (1803–1843)		
1807		Muhammad Shah Bahadur Jahan IV (titular by Rohillas)				
1808		Akbar Shah II (titular under British) (1808–1826)				
1808					12. Thakur Bhopal Singhji Berisalot (1808–1826)	
1826					13. Thakur Bakhtawar Singhji (1826–1852)	

YEAR	RULE	CENTRE	MARWAR		KHEENVSAR	NOTES
1837		Bahadur Shah II (Zafar) (1837–1852)				
1843			33. Maharaja Takhat Singhji (1843–1873)			
1852					14. Thakur Shivnath Singhji (1852–1873)	
1857	**BRITISH RAJ** (1857–1937)	**INDIAN WAR FOR INDEPENDENCE**				
1873		**BRITISH RAJ** Queen Victoria (1873–1896)		34. Maharaja Jaswant Singhji II (1873–1895)		
1875					15. Thakur Shardul Singhji (1875–1896)	
1895			35. Maharaja Sardar Singhji (1895–1911)			
1896					16. Thakur Ranjit Singhji (1896–1910)	
1901		King Edward VII				
1910		King George V (1910–1918)				

YEAR	RULE	CENTRE	MARWAR		KHEENVSAR	NOTES
1910					17. Thakur Kesari Singhji (1910–1977)	
1911				36. Maharaja Sumer Singhji (1911–1918)		
1918			37. Maharaja Umaid Singhji (1918–1947)			
1937		King George VI				
1945						Kheenvsar under the Court of Wards under Ghabana's custodianship
1947		**INDIA GAINS INDEPENDENCE**		38. Maharaja Hanwant Singhji (1947–1952)		
1947	**INDEPENDENT INDIA** (1947–Present)	Jawaharlal Nehru (1947–1952)				
1952			**39. Maharaja Gaj Singhji II** (incumbent)			
1964		Gulzarilal Nanda				
1964		Lal Bahadur Shastri				
1967		Indira Gandhi (1967–1977)				

YEAR	RULE	CENTRE	MARWAR		KHEENVSAR	NOTES
1977					18. Raja Onkar Singhji (1977–2009)	
1979		Morarji Desai				
1980		Charan Singh				
1980		Indira Gandhi				
1984		Rajiv Gandhi				
1989		V.P. Singh				
1991		Chandra Shekhar				
1991		P.V. Narasimha Rao				
1996		Atal Bihari Vajpayee				
1997		H.D. Deve Gowda				
1997		I.K. Gujral				
1998		Atal Bihari Vajpayee				
2004		Manmohan Singh (2004–2009)				
2009						Kheenvsar is re-accorded its status as a Sirayat by H.H. Maharaja Gaj Singhji II of Marwar, and its title of Raja is reinstated
2009					19. Raja Gajendra Singhji (Incumbent) (2009–Present)	
2014		**Narendra Modi** (incumbent) (2014–Present)				

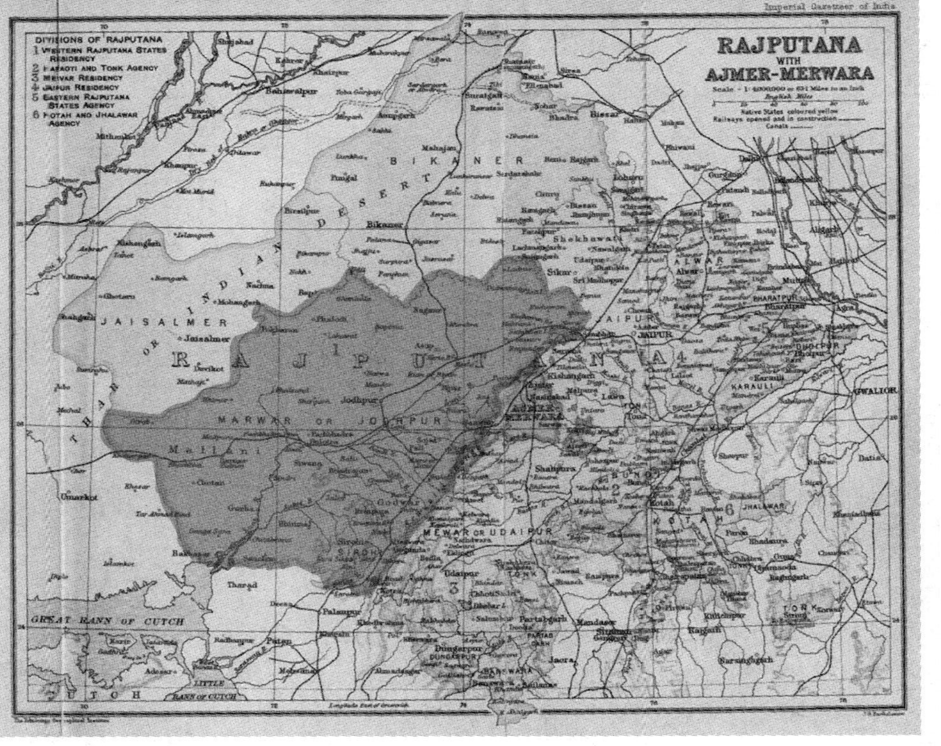

Map of Marwar, 1909

MAP OF JODHPUR STATE (MARWAR)

Scale—16 Miles to an Inch.

CENSUS 1931.

AREA AND POPULATION.

Serial No.	State or Jodhpur City or Pargana.	Area in Sq. Miles	Population.
1	2	3	4
	Marwar State.	35,016	21,25,982
1	Jodhpur City.	26	94,736
	Parganas.	34,990	20,31,246
2	Bali.	834	1,14,249
3	Bilara.	792	73,117
4	Desuri.	710	85,245
5	Didwana.	1,136	1,11,168
6	Jaitaran.	860	87,516
7	Jalore.	1,552	1,49,118
8	Jaswantpura.	1,260	1,17,176
9	Jodhpur.	2,870	1,28,621
10	Malani (Barmer).	5,670	1,78,438
11	Merta.	1,616	1,27,556
12	Nagaur.	2,608	1,42,196
13	Pachpadra.	856	31,959
14	Pali.	1,024	63,268
15	Parbatsar.	840	1,02,874
16	Phalodi.	3,573	85,121
17	Sanchore.	1,818	84,257
18	Sheo.	2,443	24,514
19	Shergarh.	1,771	63,929
20	Siwana.	760	45,676
21	Sojat.	1,172	1,17,009
22	Sambhar Marwar.	560	75,816
23	½ Sambhar Shamlat.	160	8,520

REFERENCES.

State Boundary
Pargana Boundary
J. Railway
B. B. & C. I. Railway
Metalled Road
Hills
Sand Hills
Rivers and Streams
Bunds and Tank
Pargana Head Quarters
Jodhpur-Jaipur Shamlat

Map of Marwar, 1931

The Ancestors of Rao Karamsiji

Bal hat banka Deora, kritab banka Gaud ।
Hada banka gaadh mein, Ranbanka Rathod ॥

—Agyaat Charan Kavi

Deora is a man of his words,
while Gaud is a champion of wonder.
Hada wields mighty strength,
but the champion of battles is a Rathore.

—An Anonymous Bard

Rao Sihaji (1250–1273 CE)

The Rathores are known to be descendants of the mighty Rashtrakutas, who prevailed as medieval vanquishers in central and southern India.[1] The origin of the Rathore founder, Rao Sihaji, is contested from various historical angles. Several sources claim that the ongoing pedagogical strife oscillates between the 160-kilometre-wide see-saw of Badayun on the one hand and Kannauj on the other.[2]

Kannauj often gains greater factual credibility, but a definitive nod to this conclusion is obfuscated by a third stream of historians. This stream, led by writer Manishi Maharao Raghuveer Singhji of Sirohi, adds Hastikundi to the fray.[3] Referring to ancient sources from the walls of Mehrangarh, Raghuvir Singhji points to Rao Sihaji's maternal connections with Sonigara (present-day Jalore).

This argument is challenged by archival indications that a Chauhan emperor, Maharaj Kirtipal, established Sonigara as his capital. He was the maternal grandson of Hastikundi's Rashtrakutas. Bearing these filial ties in mind, the incestuous possibility of Sonigara granting their daughter's hand to the Rashtrakutas can be rendered implausible. This speculation is further negated by Raghuvir Singhji's inability to support it with pedagogical citations.

As per the Rathore family tree published by the Mehrangarh Museum Trust on late Maharaja Umaid Singhji's centenary, Rao Sihaji was the great grandson of Rao Jaichandra from the Gaharwar dynasty that ruled over Kannauj from the 11th to the 13th centuries (the Rathore family tree has been provided in the Appendix). Mainstream historical sources connect the Gaharwars to the Rashtrakutas, and thus, to the Rathores as well.

The trilinear contest over Rao Sihaji's origins continues among historians. For now, it would be safe to say that his legendary offensive on Pali was launched from present-day Uttar Pradesh.

Rao Sihaji's famed annexation of Pali was born out of an open plea for support from Paliwal Brahmins. Rao Sihaji is believed to have been attending a holy pilgrimage in Dwarka. Upon receiving the plea, he took a detour to shield the obliged priestly caste. This fateful intervention would alter the destinies of Rao Sihaji and his progeny forever. Little did Rao Sihaji know then that amidst the arid lands of *Marudhara*, a new kingdom and the capital of his soon-to-be-established Rathore dynasty awaited his prudent discovery.

Lieutenant-Colonel James Tod, Muhnot Nainsi, Jodhpur's historical archives and diverse annals across

Marwar praise this brave founder of the Rathore dynasty. From the very beginning, Rao Sihaji consistently reinforced his newly established kingdom. However, in 1273 CE, aged 80, he perished while battling Ghiyasuddin Balban in the battle of Lakha Jhawar. A stone inscription can be found 14 miles northwest of Pali, in Beethu. It testifies to his martyrdom and to the *sati* of his queen, Rani Parvati Devi of the Solanki clan.[4]

Rao Asthanji (1273–1292 CE)

Rao Sihaji was succeeded by the eldest of his three sons, Rao Asthanji, who was born in 1212 CE. He shifted the Rathore capital to Khed, close to Pali.[5] Shortly after this, he defeated Idar's Raja Samaliya Sod and appointed his younger brother, Sonangji, as the monarch. Keeping these events in mind, one gains cognizance of Gujarat's Idariya Rathores.[6] In their lifetimes, Rao Asthanji and his brethren made a concerted effort to wield influence in the area, thereby assimilating several new provinces under Rathore hegemony.

Rao Sihaji's territorial strife for the Rathores was consolidated by his progeny. Valiant sacrifices were made on and off the battlefield, and many glories were accumulated. The clan's martial prowess earned much reverence and repute over the centuries, so much so that it merited them the title of 'Ranbanka Rathores'.

Like his father, Rao Asthanji sacrificed his life while defending his homeland. In 1291 CE, Feroz Shah Tughlaq posed a crushing defeat to a Rathore garrison of 140 men in a battle that Ojha taints as 'completely pointless'.[7]

Rao Dhuhadji (1292–1309 CE)

Rao Asthanji was avenged by his eldest son, Rao Dhuhadji, who restored Rathore dominion over 140 villages.[8] Rao Dhuhadji is said to have ascended the throne between 1291 and 1292 CE. During his reign, he consecrated his *kuldevi* Chakreshwari Mataji's statue in the village of Nagana. Today, the kuldevi is more famously known as Nagnechya Mataji, and hers is the holiest shrine for Rathores worldwide. Rao Dhuhadji gave up his life fighting the Parihars in a feud over Mandore in 1309 CE.[9]

Nagnechya Mata Temple, Nagana village, near Jodhpur;
Courtesy of Digvijay Singh

Rao Dhuhadji's younger brother, Dhandalji, conquered the erstwhile Chauhan stronghold of Kolu and is popularly known for fathering Pabuji, whose extraordinary heroism elevated him to the highest stature of the five

Rajput *pirs*. Years later, Pabuji's murder was vindicated by Rao Dhuhadji's first son, Rao Raipalji, who not only annihilated the assassin, Fardaji Bhati, but also seized 84 of his villages.

Rao Raipalji (1309–1313 CE)

A chip off the old block, Rao Raipalji's courage and altruism reminded people of his father. With immense fortitude, he vanquished the Pawars of Barmer, who administered nearly 560 villages at that time. These territories jointly came to be known as Maheva at first and later as Malani.[10] It is believed that a deadly famine hit Marwar during his reign. Rao Raipalji made no delay in alleviating the suffering of his people under his charitable leadership. His hefty donations, by means of which the kingdom's parched soils were replenished, earned him the title of *Mahirelan*, another name for Lord Indra, the Hindu God of rain. The sheer quantum of Rao Raipalji's supremacy makes it difficult for one to believe that his reign only spanned over four years (1309–1313 CE).[11]

Rao Kanpalji (1313–1323 CE)

The first of Raipalji's 14 sons, Rao Kanpalji ascended the throne in Khed after his father's demise.[12] He made his mark by expanding the Rathore kingdom right up to the Bhati state of Jaisalmer. Owing to their shared borders, the Bhatis frequently looted and pillaged areas under Rathore suzerainty. Rao Kanpalji sought to quell these extortions and thus began fortifying his borders. He assigned the bordering regions of Jaisalmer to Bhim, his primary heir. The young sentinel strongly lashed out against his defaulting neighbours and officiated a demarcation of frontiers with Jaisalmer over the Kak River. Bhim Singhji's exemplary custodianship finds references in a popular couplet:

Aadhi dharti Bhim, aadhi Lodurve dhaani.
Kaak nadi chhai seem, Rathoron ne Bhatiya.

Half of the Earth to Bhim,
the other half to the house of Lodurva[13].
The Kak River serves the border
between the Rathores and the Bhatis.

The Bhatis reacted to Bhim Singhji's stringency by allying with the region's Muslims. The impending Bhati–Muslim revolution came at the detriment of Bhim Singhji's life. Rao Kanpalji retorted by launching a counter-attack, but he too met with a similar end. The death of his father and older brother necessitated Rao Jalansiji, the deceased monarch's second son, to assume power. Bold and fearless like his kinsmen, Rao Jalansiji bore the onerous load of vendetta upon his shoulders and proceeded to follow his *dharma*.

Rao Jalansiji (1323–1328 CE)

A popular legend associated with Rao Jalansiji was that he once bestowed his guardianship upon a tree in the village of Chandni. No one was permitted to pluck a single leaf or flower from this tree. When his royal order was deliberately violated by the Sodhas of Umarkot, Rao Jalansiji confronted them in a war and emerged victorious. Upon overthrowing the Sodhas, the Rathore supremo claimed the prime ministerial *safa* of the Sodhas. In olden times, it was emblematic for the victor to imbibe a prime symbol of the vanquished force. Hence, this event paved the way for the Rathore tradition of donning safas. Similarly, the red colour in the Rathore court of arms symbolizes the red flag the Rathores had seized from Mughal control during the Battle of Ambar Champu.[14] In 1328 CE, Rao Jalansiji too went down battling the Bhati–Muslim allies that had claimed his father and brother's lives.

Rao Chadaji (1328–1344 CE)

Rao Jalansiji's first son, Rao Chadaji, grew up to avenge the Bhatis and proved to be the third consecutive Rathore ruler to be sacrificed to the same cause.

Rao Teedaji (1344–1357 CE)

This transgenerational saga of redemption continued until Rao Chadaji's eldest son eradicated his killers. The eighth scion of the Rathore dynasty, Rao Teedaji expanded his empire over Bheenmal and Lodurva. He gave up his life defending Siwana, the homeland of his nephews, Chauhan Satal and Som, in 1357.

Rao Salkhaji (1357–1374 CE)

Rao Teedaji's sons swore not to let their father's cause be rendered into oblivion. Rao Teedaji's firstborn, Rao Kanhaji, continued contesting for Maheva and successfully recaptured it from his enemies. Meanwhile, his second son, Rao Tribhuvansiji, ascended the throne at Khed. An independent *jagir* was granted to Rao Salkhaji, his third son, who seized parts of Maheva from his oldest brother. Like his brave forefathers, Rao Kanhaji went down battling Maheva's Muslim forces in 1374 CE.

Rao Veeramji (1374–1383 CE)

Rao Salkhaji's eldest son, Rao Mallinathji, inherited Maheva from his father and forcefully snatched Khed from his uncle to bequeath it to his younger brother, Rao Veeramji. His other brothers, Rao Jaitmal and Rao Shobitji, were given supreme control over Sivana and Osiyan, respectively.[15] During his reign, Rao Mallinathji cultivated Malani as a state in its own right, and he is venerated for his benevolence to date. On the banks of the Luni River in Tilwada lies a holy shrine dedicated to Malani's saintly emperor. His heroic spirit is commemorated in one of Rajasthan's biggest cattle fairs that takes place in Tilwada every year.

Rao Chundaji (1394–1423 CE)

Meanwhile, ongoing disputes with Rao Mallinathji caused Rao Veeramji to seek refuge in present-day Setarwa. He placed the custodianship of Setarwa under his first son, Rao Devrajji, and departed for Chuntisara, where he lay down his life fighting the Johiya Rajputs in 1383 CE.[16] Rao Veeramji's second son, Rao Chundaji, was all of six years when his father departed this earthly realm. The little boy spent his childhood in disguise as a commoner under the custody of Alhaji Charan in the tiny hamlet of Kalau. It was only after Rao Chundaji had attained adulthood that Alhaji Charan took him to his uncle, Rao Mallinathji, who was highly impressed by this dashing young man and granted him the charge of defending Mandore against a forthcoming attack. Rao Chundaji sought the blessings of Chamunda Mataji and commenced his duties. Later, he even built a temple for Chamunda Mataji atop a hillock near Saloni village.

Rao Chundaji established Mandore as the Rathore capital. In this context, he is fondly remembered in a Trojan horse-like war legend. The year was 1394 CE, and Mandore was under Muslim siege. On one occasion, a residing *subedar* at Mandore demanded horse fodder from the displaced Inda community.[17] The Indas belonged to the Pratihara dynasty of Agnivanshi Rajputs, and are known to have ruled over several parts of Rajasthan from the 6th to the 9th century CE. Their first capital was at Mandavyapura (present-day Mandore). The Indas were the erstwhile residents of Mandore but had been relegated to the sidelines once Muslim influence began to grow in the area.

The Indas felt insulted by such a petty appointment. To assuage their growing acrimony, they sought an alliance with Rao Chundaji, who devised a clever strategy to stealthily move his men past the fort gates. He smuggled groups of his infantrymen in the fodder supply vehicles. Once they had entered the fort complex, Rao Chundaji's army emerged from the hay sacks and ambushed the Muslims. Mandore was thus recaptured by the Rajputs. Jubilant at the triumph, the Indas appropriated Mandore Fort to the brave Rathore scion. Moreover, Ugam Singh, the Inda chieftain, even offered his daughter's hand to Rao Chundaji and permanently withdrew from Mandore, which they now considered their newly-wed daughter's home. Ugam Singh Inda and his men migrated to Balesar, where one can find a cohort of 24 villages jointly referred to as Indavati or the land of the Indas. A regional bard wrote a couplet:

Inda ro upkaar, kamdhaj man bhulo kade.
Chundo chanvri chaadh, di Mandor dayje.

Never forget this kindness bestowed upon you
by the Indas, O Rathore warrior!

Rao Chundaji fortified Mandore to the extent that it stood upright despite numerous attempts to invade it. But the ambitious ruler had loftier dreams. He sought his uncle Rao Mallinathji's backing, and in 1399 CE, they had successfully recaptured Nagaur. At the time, Gujarat's ruler, Zafar Khan, had appointed Shams Khan Dandani as Nagaur's governor, who passed it on to one of his brothers. Although his name is unknown, the Rathore army under Rao Chundaji and Rao Mallinathji clashed with Shams Khan's brother and emerged victorious.

This victory increased Rao Chundaji's confidence tenfold and drove him to unify the provinces of Khatu, Deedwana, Sambhar, Ajmer and Nadol under the Rathore dominion. However, in 1424 CE, the Pugal Bhatis joined hands with their allies from Multani and Janglu to unleash a fresh offensive on Nagaur. This formidable incursion claimed Rao Chundaji's life.

Rao Rinmalji (1427–1438 CE)

Rao Chundaji wished for the Rathore monarchy to be handed over to his sixth son, Rao Kanhaji. Even though his firstborn, Rao Rinmalji, honoured Rao Chundaji's posthumous wishes, two of his sons blatantly indulged in foul play. Within 11 months of being crowned king, Rao Kanhaji died a natural death in Mandore in 1367 CE. In Rao Rinmalji's momentary absence, Rao Sataji took undue advantage of the situation by establishing himself as the titular king for three years, from 1367 until 1370 CE. Out of turn, he put his younger brother, Rao Randhirji, in charge of important state affairs.

Now that his father's chosen son had followed him into the heavens, Rao Rinmalji considered himself the rightful heir by virtue of primogeniture. In an effort to redeem his stolen title, he sought the tutelage of his brother-in-law, Mewar's Rana Lakhaji. Rao Rinmalji's sister, Hansa Bai, was Rana Lakhaji's queen, who birthed their succeeding prince, Rana Mokalji. Upon Rana Lakhaji's untimely death in 1364 CE, Hansa Bai held the reigns of Mewar with her brother's support. Once Rana Mokalji attained maturity, he fulfilled his father's promise to his maternal uncle by launching a successful attack against Mandore in 1370 CE. Marwar's law of primogeniture was then reinstated, and Rao Rinmalji ascended the throne. Due to a fallout with Rao Sattaji, Rao Randhirji too switched sides.

After recovering Marwar from his deviant brothers, Rao Rinmalji echoed a war cry against Jaisalmer's Maharawal Lakshmanji Bhati. Upon emerging victorious, he wed the Maharawal's daughter and formed an important marital alliance with the Bhatis. He also won Jalore from Bihari Pathan Hasan Khan after a ceasefire. As of 1433 CE, the Rathore kingdom under Rao Rinmalji stretched from Mandore and Pali to Sojat, Jaitaran and Nadol. The fulfilled Rathore king embarked upon pilgrimages to Ganga and Gaya with his two sons, Jodha and Kandhal.

In the same year, Rana Mokal was assassinated by the kinsmen of his grandfather's sentry, and the traitors succeeded in capturing Chittorgarh. Upon hearing the news, Rao Rinmalji immediately set out for Mewar, establishing a six-year-old Rana Kumbha as its rightful heir while he caught hold of all of his nephew's killers, except the infamous Mahapa Panwar, who escaped, disguised as a woman.

Eventually, the conniving schemer returned to Mewar with unfinished business. He sought forgiveness from a grown Rana Kumbha, who magnanimously succumbed to his people's wishes and granted the fugitive mercy. However, just as a leopard cannot change its spots, the evil Mahapa Panwar was hatching an unfinished plot. He began poisoning Rana Kumbha's mind against his Rathore uncle. When Rao Rinmalji caught wind of the conspiracies surrounding his naïve grandnephew, he issued a warning to his Rathore scions, which Pandit Reu translates as follows:

> Nowadays, people are unlawfully soliciting Rana Kumbha against us. Since his relative lack of experience increases his gullibility, I must warn you against concurring to any invitation that I make on his behalf.

As their father had rightly predicted, Rao Jodhaji and his brethren were summoned by Rana Kumbha to his fort on numerous occasions. They ceded to their father's precautions and refused to give into Mewar's requests. Upon receiving their deliberate refusal on more than one occasion, Rana Kumbha's conspirers suspected Rao Rinmalji for Marwar's prudence and ordered for him to be assassinated. It was a dark, frigid winter night in 1438 CE when Mahapa Panwar prowled around Rao Rinmalji's chamber. He had earlier schemed with the chambermaid and bribed her to leave Rao Rinmalji's door unlatched. Once Rao Rinmalji had drifted off into deep sleep, Mahapa and his fellow assassins stealthily crept into his chamber to commit the dreadful murder. As history has repeatedly echoed, a single Rathore is enough to weigh heavily upon an entire group of adversaries. Thus, even when the brave Rathore ruler was strapped to his *charpai* and ruthlessly hacked, he stood up with the wooden bed frame and took down as many as four armed assassins before succumbing to his wounds.

This experience served as a crucial lesson for Rao Rinmalji's descendants to rely on smaller charpais such that they'd be in a better position to fight back should a similar situation arise in the future. After all, it is less challenging for a warrior to retaliate from a bed shorter than himself.

Therefore, all royal beds were deliberately made in a smaller measure than their inhabitant. The royal beds displayed in Jodhpur's Mehrangarh and Bikaner's Junagarh have similar correlations due to this story.

Shortly after this misdeed, Rana Kumbha was ridden with guilt and remorse for his treachery. Rao Rinmalji's assassination was a deep wound that forever scarred Mewar's relations with Marwar. Mewar had eternally forsaken the trust of its chief custodians. As far as Marwar was concerned, its cautionary measures increased manifold against an unscrupulous neighbour.

In his lifetime, the charitable Rao Rinmalji made several donations to the *purohit* and *charan* communities. Some notable villages given to the purohits include Kunwarda from the Jalore *pargana* and Dharmdwari and Punayata from the Pali pargana. The charans were accorded Beesawaas from the Jodhpur pargana.

Rao Jodhaji (1453–1489 CE)

The most prominent Rathore torchbearer, Rao Jodhaji, was born in 1415 CE to Rao Rinmalji and his queen, Rani Kormade Bhatiyani. The second-born Rao Jodhaji emerged as his father's undisputed favourite amongst 24 sons and, therefore, his chosen successor. After coming of age, Rao Jodhaji pursued a 15-year-long strife before reclaiming his ancestral capital of Mandore. In 1453 CE, he defeated Mewar's feudal lord, Ahada Hingola, and conquered Mandore from the Sisodias. A truly redemptive moment for all Rathores, this was only the beginning of Marwar's golden era under its most exalted king.

From the very start, Rao Jodhaji had longed to avenge his father's murder. He swore to leave no stone unturned until the last drop of Rathore blood was paid for in retribution. Enraged by the killing of his close aides by Rao Jodha's men, Rana Kumbha declared war on the Rathores. The time had arrived for Rao Jodhaji to pierce the Aravallis and hurl towards Chittorgarh to the fateful site where his father was brutally murdered in cold blood. Well aware that he lacked sufficient cavalry, the mighty Rathore ruler refused to cower in his resolve. Given the circumstances, Rao Jodhaji resorted to transporting his army via bullock carts. The mere sight of the mighty Rathore army advancing on Chittorgarh made the Rana's army shudder and flee.

Accompanied by his valiant men, Rao Jodhaji surrounded Chittorgarh from all sides and set fire to the fort gates. Making his way in, he prostrated at the door of the chamber in which his late father was assassinated. A contemporary poet, Gadan Pasait, has showered his beloved monarch with much adulation in his work, *Jodhayan*, which translates as follows:

Such was the gist of Jodha
that without horses, you unconventionally crossed the
Aravallis to attack the mighty fort of Chittor.
Hearing your war cry caused abortions
in the women of Mewar.
Oh! Descendent of Chunda,
You burnt down the gates of Mewar
and worshipped the chambers of your great father.

After his Chittorgarh vendetta, Rao Jodhaji ordered his men to pillage Mewar's villages. Rana Kumbha retorted by attacking Narlai with his army. Here, he found Rao Jodhaji and his army ready for combat. Before the two sides delved into another skirmish, better judgement prevailed, and their rulers entered a concordat. According to this agreement, all land covered by *babool* trees went to Marwar, whereas Mewar retained the realm of the *baanwal* trees. A couplet narrates this arrangement:

Maho maas basi taala firaaya.
Tare atha aawal aawal Rana ra ne
baanwal baanwal Rao ra.

In the lunar month of Maagh,
a treatise is thus formed (whereby)
the land with bawal (acacia) trees
are the Rao's (Marwar) and
the land with the amla (mango) trees
of the Rana (Mewar).

Rao Jodhaji's coronation occurred in 1439 CE when he was affectionately felicitated by his eldest brother, Akhyaraj. He anointed the new sovereign's forehead with the crimson blood of his freshly slashed thumb. The following year, Rao Jodhaji laid the foundation for a fort on the Chidiyatoonk hillock. Around eight kilometres south of Mandore, this iconic fort came to be known as Mehrangarh or the fort of the sun, signifying the *Suryavanshi* origin of the Rathores.

Thus, the new Rathore capital, the city of Rao Jodha or Jodhpur, came into being. He relocated his ancestral deity, Chamunda Mataji, from her erstwhile abode in Mandore and consecrated her temple in Mehrangarh's Chawda Burj.

Rao Jodhaji is venerated and adored by one and all for being the charitable founding father of the present Rathore capital. He is also considered the first leader who consolidated Marwar as the predominant homeland of the Rathores. His industriousness and foresight led to his recognition as a true pioneer of his era. In their lifetimes, Rao Jodhaji and his kinsmen established as many as nine Rathore principalities across the Indian subcontinent. His exemplary contributions to Marwar and the Rajput fraternity are prided over by Kshatriyas worldwide. The glorious founder of Jodhpur remains immortalized in the hearts of his people. Mounted atop his stallion, his statue overlooks Mehrangarh and places the city of Jodhpur under his divine providence.

Rao Jodha's statue; Courtesy of Digvijay Singh

Here is one of the numerous songs sung in Rao Jodha's praise:

Jin din Jodh janamiya, jas thaal vajaaya.
Jei sir chatra namiya ne chatra namasya.
Bundi naal Bandhi diye Raav Rinmal jaaya.
Kachawa Bhatiya naler vadaaya.
Sumasaat susara sau pesle aaya.
Baleesa Rao Adhpati Chauhaan namaaya.
Jalore jokha khamiya mil soje laaya.
Satre cha sihra iya sir ank samaaya.
Ghaneraav ujaariya Gundocho rav sahaaya
Nadol aaya nehasiya rin dhol ghuraaya.
Kiya parvada Rathore chand dhadhi gaaya.
Jodhe ganjam chediya peechole paaya.

The day Rao Jodhaji was born,
cymbals were clashed in victory.
Even those who never faced defeat,

bent their heads in front of Rao Jodhaji.
The brave son of Rao Rinmalji
extended his influence up to Bundi.
The Kachhwaha and Bhati clans
solicited him into wedlock with their princesses.
He vanquished the Balochis and Chauhans.
He conquered Sojat,
Even Jalore had to bow down under his triumph.
He rescued Rathores from Ghanerao
and rehabilitated them in Gundoj.
The war trumpets in Nadol cried at the site
of Rao Jodhaji coming to fight Rana Kumbha's army.
Dhadhi Ramchandra sings songs of the
brave Rao Jodhaji.
So mighty was he that he pushed
Rana Kumbha's Mewar army back to Lake Pichola.

Once, when he embarked on a pilgrimage to Gaya in 1461 CE, Rao Jodhaji chanced upon a meeting with the then emperor of Delhi, Bahlul Khan Lodi, in Agra. The Lodi king showered his deference on Rao Jodhaji and pledged him his support whereby he would abolish religious taxes on Hindu and Buddhist pilgrims. On this journey, he also befriended Jaunpur's last king, Husain Shah. A strong friendship was forged between the two, and Rao Jodhaji extended the Shah his support against miscreant Pathans around Gwalior. Rao Jodha remained true to his word, so much so that he never spared the Shah's enemies. In his forthcoming pilgrimages to Dwarka, Prayag (present-day Prayagraj) and Kashi (present-day Varanasi), he wreaked havoc upon Jaunpur's enemies whenever he happened to spot them.

After three glorious decades of his reign, Rao Jodhaji drew his last breath on 6 April 1489 CE. In a legacy spanning 73 years, Rao Jodhaji was an intelligent and judicious ruler. His unparalleled achievements made him the brightest star in the Rathore constellation. When the Delhi Sultanate began crumbling, provincial governors across Gujarat, Malwa, Jaunpur and Multan began contesting for sovereign power. The Rathore head made prudent use of these squabbles and focused on increasing his stronghold over Marwar. Little did Delhi and its neighbours notice that while they were busy wrestling for power, the visionary leader had stretched his empire to the far extents of Jaisalmer in the west, Hisar in the north and the Aravallis in the south.

Rao Jodhaji

Understandably, the conquest of such vast expanses came with the immense responsibility of their governance. To single-handedly govern such a vast territory proved challenging even for a ruler of Rao Jodhaji's calibre. As a result, he encouraged his progeny to consolidate their father's dominion by establishing their own kingdoms under Rathore sovereignty.

In all, Rao Jodhaji's kindred established eleven principalities.

Ruler	*Principality (year established)*
Rao Chundaji (son of Rao Veeramji)	Marwar, Rajasthan (1395 CE)
Rao Bikaji (son of Rao Jodhaji)	Bikaner, Rajasthan (1485 CE)
Rao Kishan Singhji (son of Mota Raja Udai Singhji)	Kishangarh, Rajasthan (1552 CE)
Raja Jai Singhji (son of Kunwar Pratap Singhji, grandson of Raja Chhatrasal Singhji)	Sailana, Madhya Pradesh (1730 CE)
Raja Keshavdasji	Sitamau, Madhya Pradesh (1701 CE)
Raja Ratan Singhji (son of Rao Maheshdasji, grandson of Kunwar Dalpat Singhji and great grandson of Mota Raja Udai Singhji)	Ratlam, Madhya Pradesh (1652 CE)
Rao Jagannath Singhji (descendant of Rao Maldeoji)	Amjhera, Madhya Pradesh (1604 CE)

Raja Keshavdasji (descendant of Varsinghji, son of Rao Jodhaji), was granted Jhabua as its Raja by the then emperor Jahangir)	Jhabua, Madhya Pradesh (1584 CE)
Rao Sonagji (son of Rao Sihaji)	Idar, Gujarat (1275 CE)
Rao Karamsiji (son of Rao Jodhaji)	Kheenvsar, Rajasthan (1523 CE)
Rao Dudaji (son of Rao Jodhaji)	Merta, Rajasthan (1480 CE)

The ninth son of Rao Jodhaji grew to establish a scintillating legacy of the Karamsot Rathores. In 1523 CE, the young prince made an overnight march with his army, some 90 kilometres northeast of Jodhpur. A jagged rock pressed beneath his head as he lay down to rest. When the restless night ended, he awoke to a miraculous discovery. It was no ordinary rock but a Shiva linga-shaped stone protruding from the earth. Interpreting this as a sign of blessing from the Almighty, he followed the divine ordinance to establish his kingdom on the land that surrounded the sacred linga.

1

Rao Karamsiji

The Fountainhead

The year was 1440 CE when Rao Jodhaji and his wife, Rani Purade Bhatiyaniji of Jaisalmer, birthed a bright-eyed boy as their ninth scion.[1] When correlated with the Gregorian calendar, their infant was born at the cusp of the morning and afternoon hours on Thursday, 8 December 1440. His was no ordinary birth. This fateful month of Marghashirsha in the Hindu calendar had heralded a birth that was to permanently alter the annals of history. The ninth scion of Rao Jodha was born with the destiny of establishing a Rathore sub-dynasty of his own. He is immortalized as Rao Karamsiji, and his progeny flourishes under his banner as Karamsots—the kindred of Karamsiji.

After occupying Mandore in 1453 CE, Rao Jodhaji split his army into three parts.

The first two parts were sent to fortify Mandore and Kosana. He led the third division to launch an attack on Chaukdi. Rao Karamsiji was only 12 years old when he accompanied his father on this campaign.[2]

Rao Karamsiji was a little boy when Marwar recaptured Mandore from the Rana of Mewar. Its 12 year-old siege over Mandore ended with Rao Jodha and his army recapturing it in 1453 CE. In a similar feat, the Rathores were successful in their ambushes at Kosana and Chaukdi, causing the Ranas to scuttle with their men.

Rao Karamsiji's inborn leadership skills and exemplary war tactics earned him his father's deep appreciation, so much so that Rao Jodhaji appointed him the prime supervisor to oversee the construction of his newly sanctioned fort complex, Mehrangarh. One of its gates still echoes a timeless story related to this young custodian.

The Boon of Sage Chidiyanathji

Rao Jodhaji ordered Mehrangarh's construction to commence on 12 May 1459. Much of the fort's development was placed under the watchful eye of Rao Karamsiji, who was only nineteen years old at the time. During the initial stages of masonry, a unique challenge arose. It wasn't a geographical fissure or uneven elevation that stood in the way. Instead, Rao Jodhaji's entourage found a sage deep in meditation. It was the hermitage of the renowned Sage Chidiyanathji. Because Rao Jodhaji himself had sanctioned the maps that directed Mehrangarh's walls to pass through the famed hermit's dwelling, Sage Chidiyanathji's divine penance came to an abrupt halt.

Raipalji, one of Rao Jodha's sons, committed the folly of confronting an embittered hermit. In the heat of the moment, the young prince lost his composure, and his brazenness triggered the sage's wrath. Chidiyanathji tossed the blazing sacrificial embers into his sack, but they seemed placid compared to his simmering temper. Just as he was beginning to vacate the site in a huff, the sage couldn't help but castigate Raipalji for his insolence, 'You have interrupted my penance and dared to dislodge me for the sake of a wall. I curse you for your utter disrespect and lack of consideration. May your fort never attain completion and be frequented by droughts. As for you, your progeny shall most certainly perish!'

News of this incident swiftly reached Rao Karamsiji, who was then supervising development in a neighbouring section of the fort. Without a moment's delay, he rushed to beg the wrathful sage for mercy. He fell on his feet and expressed profuse remorse on behalf of his errant brother. Not long after Rao Karamsiji's intervention, Rao Jodhaji also expressed his apologies and sanctified the sage's hermitage. As per his directives, a Shivalinga was consecrated and the natural fountain was allowed to flow its natural course through the holy cave before ending in a cistern. This cistern continues to proffer water to its visitors at Mehrangarh.

Chidiyanath ji's sthaan

Chidiyanath ji's cave

With this gesture, Rao Jodhaji succeeded in placating Chidiyanathji. In turn, the sage blessed him and his empire to flourish and proclaimed that so long as Rao Jodhaji's dynasty abided by moral principles of conduct, Marwar would continue to harvest water even amidst the fiercest of droughts. However, unlike the rest of his brothers, Prince Raipalji wasn't spared the holy wrath conferred upon him. His lineage remained confined to three and a half jagirs.

The Birth of the Karamsot Empire

Each of Rao Jodhaji's sons earned the illustrious title of Rao by virtue of establishing their respective kingdoms. However, their quests are yet to be accorded due credit and recognition in mainstream history.

Like his brothers, Rao Karamsiji set out to commence his independent pursuit. It is believed that the young prince was disheartened upon receiving a sum of 5,000 rupees from his father, which he considered a paltry contribution, even in those days. Although Rao Karamsiji departed without seeking his father's blessings, Rao Jodha ensured that he was accompanied by 125 horse cavalrymen, 72 camel cavalrymen, 35 bullock carts and his cherished elephant, Manak.

The royal entourage first halted at Peepaad, where Rao Karamsiji and his men were hosted by a close ally, Serpoji Sujawat. By the fourth day of their stay, Rao Karamsiji's army had obtained a bounty worth 1,25,000 rupees and set up camp in Chaukdi. It was atop the hillock of this village that Rao Karamsiji envisioned his fort.

Just then, a strange event occurred.

To build their new fort in Chaukdi, Rao Karamsiji's men began laying its foundations. They toiled under the scorching sun for many days, but come night-time, a supernatural, invisible force would cause the walls to crumble down. Day after day, the men would erect the walls, only for their efforts to be negated overnight. This strange interplay continued until Rao Karamsiji finally relented and sought a religious ordinance with Kalka Mataji, the presiding deity of the region.

It was after much divine penance that the goddess appeared before Rao Karamsiji and stated the impossibility of his vision coming to life atop her hillock. Instead, she directed him to lay the foundations of his future abode at Nadsar, some 90 kilometres northeast of Jodhpur.

Following this sacred prophecy, Rao Karamsiji departed for Nadsar, where he spent an entire year serving its inhabitants in an eager attempt to appease the goddess. He even replenished Nadsar's residents with food and water and constructed a temple dedicated to Kalka Mataji.

During this migratory year, Rao Karamsiji's animosity with the Khanzada of Nagaur escalated into a bitter ambush. Nagaur's Khanzada not only suffered a crushing defeat but also lost 122 horses to the triumphant son of Rao Jodhaji. The latter made a subsequent offensive against Jayal, whose resident, Mohabam Singh Kheechi, made him a peace offering of 7,000 rupees. Kavi Jaan has stated that Kheenvsar and Aasop were taken by Rao Karamsiji after a treatise with the Khanzada of Nagaur, but this claim has been refuted due to a lack of substantial evidence.[3]

The story of Kheenvsar's inception lies amidst contesting narratives. According to Reu, Rao Karamsiji established his kingdom in Kheenvsar and Aasop somewhere between 1467 and 1489 CE.[4] In contrast, Rao Sohan Singhji states that Kheenvsar was obtained after Rao Karamsiji's victory over Kheenvsar's then feudal lord, Bhojrajji Malingiya, in 1494 CE.

G.R. Parihar argues that Rao Karamsiji laid the foundations of his empire before 1486 CE, which was the year his brothers, Rao Bikaji and Rao Dudaji, established Bikaner and Merta, respectively.[5]

The late Thakur Bhanwar Singhji of Tantawas contradicts Parihar and asserts that Rao Karamsiji had ventured out of Jodhpur with his older brother, Rao Bikaji.[6] During their overnight halt in Beerai, the partially asleep Rao Karamsiji felt something prodding against his head. That night, Kalka Mataji appeared in his dream and commanded him to establish his empire on the soil upon which he lay. The following morning, he awoke to discover that the protrusion wasn't any ordinary rock but a holy Shivalinga. Astounded by this coincidence, Rao Karamsiji confided in his brother, Rao Bikaji, and their uncle, Kandalji. They concurred that this dream was a cosmic sign, a divine ordinance from Kalka Mataji. Rao Bikaji advised his younger brother to adhere to the Goddess's divine intervention and establish his kingdom there.

Thus, Rao Karamsiji diverged from his older brother's military procession, which proceeded to establish Bikaner around 150 kilometres north of Kheenvsar. Shortly afterwards, Rao Karamsiji made another overnight halt at Kheenvsar, when this mysterious incident replayed in his dreams.

By now, any residual doubts in Rao Karamsiji's mind had been washed away. He was certain that this message was supernatural. He resolved to establish his permanent dwelling by the region's concavity, where monsoon winds condensed into a lake. He named his new abode Kshemsar, which can be translated into a lake (sar) that preludes safety and well-being (kshem). Over the centuries, rural dialect eroded his supreme nomenclature, and the place gradually came to be pronounced as Kheenvsar.

The Beerai Rock in the Shiva Temple, Kheenvsar

Even today, Lord Baijnathji is venerated in Kheenvsar in the form of the rock that Rao Karamsiji had encountered. This Shivalinga continues to reign supreme in a temple within Kheenvsar Fort. Over the many centuries since Rao Karamsiji's foundation of the Karamsot empire, Mahadev's holy monolith safeguards the Karamsots as their *ishtadevata* or presiding deity.

In its 500-year-long history, Kheenvsar emerged as Marwar's forthright defenders, fighting countless wars in its name. Rao Karamsiji gave up his life on the battlegrounds of Narnaul in present-day Haryana. Alongside him lay the slain Rao Lunkaranji of Bikaner. Rao Karamsiji's widowed queens committed sati in Aasop in a collective bid to defend their honour.

Karamsiji's Numerous Expeditions

Chaapar Dronpur Offensive I

When news of his younger brother Kandalji's murder by Sarang Khan reached Rao Jodhaji's ears, he declared war against the miscreant.[7] Rao Bikaji and Rao Karamsiji joined their father in avenging their deceased uncle. Unsurprisingly, Rathore sovereignty prevailed over Chaapar Dronpur (present-day Churu), and their brother, Beedaji, was made the primordial custodian of the province. A triumphant Rao Jodhaji was retreating to Jodhpur with his sons when he promised to reward Rao Bikaji with some precious family heirlooms. Rao Karamsiji stood witness to his father's commitment, which would soon be dishonoured by Jodhpur's new heir, Rao Sujaji.

Rao Bikaji's Jodhpur Offensive

Rao Jodhaji died in 1489 CE and was succeeded by his son, Rao Satalji. However, due to his untimely death within 2 years of being coronated, Rao Satalji's brother, Rao Sujaji, was appointed as the King of Marwar in 1491 CE. Shortly afterwards, Rao Sujaji was served a reminder from Bikaner. He was to fulfil their father's promise of granting Rao Bikaji certain family heirlooms, but he flatly refused to part with them. Rao Sujaji's dishonourable act enraged Rao Bikaji, and the situation took an acute turn. A matter that was already personal escalated into a question of pride. Bikaner prepared to acquire its late father's heirlooms at any cost, even if it meant going to war against Jodhpur. The threat of an impending offensive loomed large over Marwar.

Owing to his cordial relations with Rao Bikaji, Rao Karamsiji hurried to broker peace between his brothers. He eventually succeeded, and the two Raos reconciled. At the behest of their father's widowed queen, Rani Jasmadeji, the heirlooms promised to him were handed over to Rao Bikaji and he returned a happy man.[8]

This marked the first amongst Rao Karamsiji's many mediations for peace. Like the Karamsot founder, his progeny continued to uphold the cause of Rathore unity. In fact, Rao Karamsiji's patriotic lineage continues to be credited by the present heads of Marwar and Bikaner as prominent harbingers of peace in Marwar.

Chaapar Dronpur Offensive II and the War of Dhosi

When Rao Bikaji's successor, Rao Lunkaranji, pursued Fatehpur and Chayalwada in 1512 CE, Rao Karamsiji lent him his vehement support. The uncle–nephew duo jointly unfurled Bikaner's flag at Kanthaliya, Deedwana, Narhan and Sivana. Within a decade and a half, they significantly expanded Bikaner's territories. The time was ripe to attempt their master stroke on the fertile lands of Chaapar Dronpur.

When its presiding ruler, Rao Kalyanmalji Beedawat[9], anticipated this potential invasion, he withdrew his support from Rao Lunkaranji's cavalcade towards Narnaul. Other allies, such as Raimalji and Rao Harji Bhati, followed suit because they suspected that the conquered lands would be reserved exclusively for the Rathores. Worse still, they switched sides and joined the defending army at Narnaul, which was commanded by a Lodi chieftain, Nawab Sheru Abi Mira.

Deserted by his own men, Rao Lunkaranji remained under the shelter of Rao Karamsiji, and the two set up their camp 12 kilometres west of Narnaul in a place called Dhosi. The fateful war was fought on 28 June 1526, when several traitors fled like cowards upon seeing the Rathore advance.[10] Even though they stood outnumbered, Rao Karamsiji and Rao Lunkaranji confronted Nawab Sheru Abi's army. The brave warriors fought relentlessly under the scorching summer sun and were eventually slain. Narnaul's parched soil was splattered with Rathore blood and martyrdom.

A Vindication of Rathore History

Rao Karamsiji paid dearly for his unwavering loyalty towards his clansmen. His noble intentions caused him to overlook the price that his military preoccupation would incur on Kheenvsar, which lay neglected in his absence.

Even though Rao Jodhaji had accorded each of his son's kingdoms the rank of Marwar's prime sirayats, the sovereign statuses of Kheenvsar, Merta and Bikaner were deliberately compromised by his successor, Rao Maldeo. Well aware that his brethren were diverted in their various military campaigns, he played the situation to his selfish advantage and usurped their territories. Ultimately, only Bikaner survived Rao Maldeo's sabotage that rendered the sirayats as jagirs. Because of this, Kheenvsar and Merta, too, fell from their ranks and were wrongly integrated into Marwar as mere jagirs.

Kheenvsar's resounding pleas against this blatant injustice echo across the annals of history.

A famous African proverb says, 'Until the lions have their own historians, tales of the hunt shall always glorify the hunter.' This applies more broadly to Rajput historiography as well, given the relative absence of the clan's narratives in historical discourses. In Kheenvsar's context, it would be a misapprehension on one's part to interpret this discrediting of history as a benign archival folly. In fact, what began as a deliberate falsification of Kheenvsar's inferior rank by an insecure Rao Maldeo gradually solidified into a plausible myth. This myth permeated public conscience over centuries and legitimized subsequent historical misrepresentations. As a matter of fact, fallacies birthed by conspiracies, if repeatedly cited, end up undermining the truth.

To cite examples from the 17th and 19th centuries, the records of Muhnot Nainsi during the reign of Jodhpur's Rao Jaswant Singhji I (1638–1678 CE) and those of Bankidas under Rao Mansinghji (1803–1843 CE) generate bizarre notions of Rao Karamsiji's acquisition of Kheenvsar. According to their records, the young prince gained Kheenvsar as a result of his sister, Bhaga Bai's, marriage to the Nawab of Nagaur.

Kavi Jaan, in his anthology *Kayam Khan Raasa*, elevates Nainsi and Bankidas's interpretations to an entirely different level of absurdity.[11] He concocts a story according to which the growing power of Nagaur's *nawab* intimidated Rao Jodhaji to such an extent that in a placatory gesture, he proffered his daughter's hand to the nawab. This preposterous narrative claims that upon being refused by the nawab, the Rathore princess's proposal was then presented to Shams Khan, a *Kayamkhani* from Jhunjhunu. This story then states that Shams Khan obliged Rao Jodhaji on the sole condition that he send the Rathore bride on her palanquin to the nawab's homeland and spare him the commute.

These claims are flouted by contemporary historians such as Reu and Ojha, as well as by Dr Dasharatha Sharma, Agarchand Nahata and Bhanwarlal Nahata, who are amongst the primary editors of *Kayam Khan Raasa*.[12] In 1953 CE, they jointly refuted these historiographical conspiracies on two grounds. First, no historical records or archives suggest the slightest possibility of Rao Jodha's subservience to mightier kings. If even the Ranas of Mewar couldn't restrain Rao Jodhaji, the Nawab of Nagaur didn't stand a chance. Second, Fateh Khan served as Nagaur's nawab during Rao Jodha's time. Thus, Saleh Khan being touted as the nawab is an obvious fabrication.

Several historians of high repute have unanimously rejected the aforementioned historical misrepresentations as false and concurred that Rao Karamsiji attained Kheenvsar by means of military strife.[13] Sometime around 1467 CE, it is believed that Rao Jodhaji gained control over Nagaur from Kayamkhani Fatankhan, who then fled to Jhunjhunu.[14] Marwar's triumphant Rao offered the provinces of Nadsar and Aasop to his sons, Rao Karamsiji and Raipalji, respectively. Rao Karamsiji's sovereign title was officiated by Rao Jodhaji soon after Nagaur's integration into Marwar in 1467 CE.

Therefore, it can be soundly concluded that these historiographical distortions were augmented by envious contemporaries of the Rathores, who sought to seek reassurance by tarnishing the mighty Rathores' image. Contrary to these petty schemes, age-old bards highlight Rao Karamsiji's selfless service to his clan and people.

The Karamsot Kindred

When it comes to a clear documentation of Rao Karamsiji's kindred, historical archives remain ambiguous. According to some accounts, he married thrice, whereas others claim that the Karamsot founder had four, five and even six wives.[15] The radical variation of his family tree can be immensely baffling to the unsuspecting reader; hence, it is safe to follow the traditionally accepted ambiguity that Rao Karamsiji established conjugal ties with the princesses of the Hada, Solanki, Lakhawat and Sodha clans. Most historical records concur with this index and mention that his successor, Rao Pichyaansiji, was born to his Hada queen, Rani Prem Kanwar.

The temple commissioned by Rani Prem Kanwar in Aasop

She is said to have consecrated a temple in Aasop, for which she contributed a handsome sum of 17,000 rupees. Sometime during the spring of 1501 CE, Rani Prem Kanwar is believed to have donated a cow and offered several priests a ceremonial feast as a homage to the new temple.

Until his martyrdom, Rao Karamsiji's entire family resided in Aasop, and his Hada and Solanki queens committed sati there. A *chhatri* to the right side of Aasop fort's gate is dedicated to their sacrifice.

Among Rao Jodhaji's sons, Rao Karamsiji is lauded by numerous historians as the most virtuous, brotherly and affectionate. He loyally devoted himself to his clan and put forth his life in defence of his motherland. He was a spirited and fiery warrior of 86 years when he fought the battle of Narnaul. Rao Karamsiji's brilliance as a warrior goes hand in hand with his political wisdom, with historians placing special emphasis on his judicial and amicable nature. A posthumous chhatri dedicated to him stands between Dhosi and Narnaul, upon the very soil where the brave Karamsot founder lay down his life.

2

Rao Pichyaansiji

Like Father, Like Son

Long after the fountainhead of all Karamsots was slain in the distant land of Dhosi, his spirited legacy remained immortalized in an entire lineage of bravehearts known as the Karamsot Rathores. Incidentally, Rao Karamsiji wasn't the sole Karamsot defending Marwar's flag in Narnaul. The second Karamsot ruler, Rao Pichyaansiji, fought alongside his progenitor as a young prince and grew up to be a chip off the old block. Rao Pichyaansiji was born in 1486 CE to Rao Karamsiji's Hada queen, Prem Kanwar.[1] The second Karamsot ruler dutifully upheld his family's sacrificial ethos in the numerous trials and tribulations he faced during his illustrious career. As subsequent war accounts proved, Rao Pichyaansiji stayed true to his people and served his clan until his dying day.

The Battle of Raati Ghati

After Babar's spectacular victory over Hindustan, the Mughal empire began to weaken under the reign of his successor, Humayun. Seizing this situation to his advantage, the deceased king's second son and Humayun's younger brother, Kamran Mirza, captured Lahore, Punjab, Kandahar and Ghazni. Even after these magnificent conquests, the scheming prince yearned for more. His ravenous eyes began to leer at Rao Bikaji's desert solitaire, Bikaner. Thus, Kamran's army advanced westwards and acquired the neighbouring area of Bhatner (present-day Bikaner) in the October of 1534 CE. Their early victory boosted Kamran's morale to the verge of overconfidence, and his army hastily encompassed Bikaner's Junagadh fort.

Kamran's unwarranted offensive was challenged by a heroic Rathore garrison at the neighbouring war ground of Raati Ghati. Bikaner's incumbent ruler, Rao Jaitsiji, commanded the defending force along with his band of brothers, including Rao Pichyaansiji and his younger sibling, Prithvirajji. Their unassailable war strategies forced Kamran's army to retreat to Lahore and never lay eyes on Bikaner again. Dayaldas noted an occurrence that corresponds with this strife. He writes, 'The manner in which Kamran retreated to flee was so hasty that he left behind a deserted Mughal army. His petrified heel struck the horse, which galloped forward with such furore that his combat helmet flew off and was swept away by the wind. The terrified Mughal failed to muster any courage to retrieve it from the ground upon which it fell.'[2]

To this day, Kamran Mirza's fabled helmet remains in the possession of ballad mongers in a village called Chautriya, the historic place where it had fallen.

The victorious Rao Jaitsiji honoured each one of his men with a horse to convey his gratitude. Rao Pichyaansiji's indomitable prowess was felicitated with him being awarded with Pareva, the best stallion whose speed is equated with the fastest gust of wind. Rao Pichyaansiji fought Kamran's army astride a swift silverish steed of high pedigree. A Dingala poem in a historical compilation commissioned by Rao Jaitsiji showers much praise on him[3]:

Parevai dhaapatai ati pai,
neeghsah dhara tiripi nihai.
Pichyaansina chadiyu abhi pana,
moogli ghada bhradviva maana.

The horse 'Parewa' whose feet hit the earth
while running very fast.
Pichyaansiji rode on such a horse
with his arms raised to crush the
pride of the Mughal army.

During Rao Pichyaansiji's military campaigns, Kheenvsar remained under the secure custodianship of his son, Maheshdasji. No sooner had the victorious king made a brief sojourn in Kheenvsar than Marwar summoned him once again. This time, Jodhpur's Rao Maldeo had announced a vendetta in Kumbhalgarh.

The Kumbhalgarh Vendetta

A timeless saying goes, all is fair in love and war. History stands testament to this and is rife with tales of legendary wars fought in the name of love. Be it the Trojan War for Helen or the War of Actium for Cleopatra, tales of love transforming into armed vendettas are historical clichés worldwide, and Rajput history, too, is replete with such encounters.

One of India's most iconic tales is based in the erstwhile kingdom of Mewar and its queen, Rani Padmavati.[4] In the 14th century, Delhi's Sultan Alauddin Khalji is believed to have become so utterly crazed and obsessed over rumours of Rani Padmavati's beauty that he sought to acquire her. What ensued was his offensive against Mewar. The defending ruler and Rani Padmavati's husband, Rana Ratan Singhji, put up a valiant defence against Khalji, only to be wiped out by the salacious sultan. When no hope remained, Rani Padmavati and 1,600 other women performed *jauhar* to defend their honour against the barbaric Khalji.

History repeated itself with Rana Ratan Singh and Rani Padmavati's succession, albeit as an intra-communal vendetta that was far less gruesome.

An internal dispute had forced Jait Singh, a noble

from Udaipur, to flee. Banished from his homeland, he sought Rao Maldeo's guardianship in the neighbouring Marwar. The generous king placed Jait Singh under his providence and granted him the jagir of Khairwa. Rao Maldeo even forged familial ties with Jait Singh by marrying his older daughter, Swaroop Devi.[5] The newly-wed king was soaked in nuptial bliss when he visited his father-in-law in Khairwa. There, Rao Maldeo was introduced to his sister-in-law, whose beauty threw the Maharaja into deep rapture. Hopelessly in love, Rao Maldeo couldn't help but request Jait Singh for his younger daughter's hand as well.

Jait Singh was now caught in a tricky situation. He could not offend his patron and now son-in-law Rao Maldeo, whose grace had put a roof over his head. So, he requested for some time to make preparations for their wedding. No sooner had his reassured son-in-law returned to Jodhpur than Jait Singh hurriedly migrated with his family to Kumbhalgarh, where he bequeathed his damsel to Mewar's Rana Uday Singh.

News of Jait Singh's escape soon travelled to Marwar. With an enraged mind and a wounded ego, Rao Maldeo commanded an assault on Kumbhalgarh under Rao Pichyaansiji's leadership. After all, how could his chosen bride be handed over to his contemporary in the rival kingdom of Mewar? That too by his own father-in-law whom he had protected? The Jodhpur *durbar* couldn't bear this insult. Thus, in order to resurrect its pride, Rao Maldeo's army attacked Mewar in 1540 CE. The skirmish ensued until the Rana's army eventually blockaded Rao Maldeo's men from advancing towards Kumbhalgarh.

Despite the impasse, Rao Pichyaansiji did not return to Jodhpur empty handed. According to Reu's accounts, he had commanded his army to aggressively supersede the Godwad and Khairwa provinces from Mewar, thus expanding Marwar's dominion over a highly strategic territory in Rao Maldeo's favour.[6]

Thakur Chotu Singhji Devra of Devatra illustrates Rao Maldeo's Kumbhalgarh vendetta in a satirical verse: 'Jhaad kaatiya, Jhaali na mili', meaning 'Rao Maldeo burnt down the foliage around Kumbhalgarh's hills, but in vain for he couldn't find the Jhala princess.'

Saubhagya Singh Shekhawat praises Rao Pichyaansiji's valour in a song recounting how he browbeat Mewar's Rana Kumbha at Nadol, forcing him into a hasty retreat.[7]

The Battle of Giri-Sumel

If one was to name the most definitive battle of Rathore history, the battle of Giri-Sumel was it. This iconic battle remains unprecedented in its sheer quantum of participation and the bereavements that followed. Unlike the battle of Haldighati, which receives due historical attention, the battle of Giri-Sumel continues to lurk in the shadows of historical recollection. It could be argued that Indian historiography was altered against the Rajputs by the large-scale socialist propaganda heralded by the newly-independent Indian state under Jawaharlal Nehru and his daughter, Indira Gandhi. Unfortunately, this post-independence revisionism neglected sizeable churns of Rajput history and systematically denied India's erstwhile nobility their due historical representation.

It is no coincidence that India's Rajputs were reduced to a disunited community of British Raj apologists. Pre colonial invasions are often blamed upon the collective failure of India's princely states. Socialist revisions of textbook history, the subsequent abolition of titles and privy purposes were gusts of the same tempest. Vestiges of Rajput stereotypes by socialist agendas can be found in mainstream cinema and literature of post-independence India, with tropes of extorting, aloof, debaucherous and entitled Rajputs finding numerous representations on and off celluloid.

These deliberate sabotages notwithstanding, it isn't too late to reclaim one's narrative by initiating authentic representation from within the community. This stands true, not just for pedagogical mediums but also for mainstream cinema, art and subaltern historiographies. The ever brilliant Shashi Tharoor writes with his profound wisdom, 'You can't revenge yourself upon history, history is its own revenge'.[8] Tharoor's implication reverberates in the African proverb mentioned in the previous chapter, 'Until the lions have their own historians, tales of the hunt shall always glorify the hunter.' Perhaps the time has come for lions to have their own historians or, better still, for lions to take charge of their own historiographies (on a side note, it is difficult to ignore the coincidence of many Rajput surnames corresponding with the lion and tiger).[9]

Returning to the battle of Giri-Sumel, this clash between Sher Shah Suri and Rao Maldeo went down in history as one of the largest and fiercest battles in Rajput annals. At Giri-Sumel, 12,000 Rajputs contended with 1,20,000 Afghans. The forces driving the impending carnage at Giri-Sumel were twofold.

Rao Maldeo

On the one hand was Sher Shah Suri's swelling ambition to acquire Rajputana. On the other hand, Rao Maldeo sought territorial expansion and forcefully annexed Merta from Rao Veeramdevji and Bikaner from Rao Jaitsi in 1542 CE.

To regain their lost kingdoms, Rao Veeramdevji and Bikaner's new ruler, Rao Kalyanmalji, sought an alliance with Rao Maldeo's formidable enemy. The two exiled kings travelled to Delhi to solicit Sher Shah Suri's support. The latter struck while the iron was hot and acted upon his long-standing ambition to overthrow the Rathore king. This newly obtained justification of moral righteousness added another motive to Sher Shah's preparation for war.

A hint of Sher Shah's designs reached Rao Kumpaji, who was presiding over Deedwana at the time.[10] Alarmed at the imminent danger, he immediately sent a messenger to alert Rao Maldeo. Beholden to Rao Kumpaji for his swift vigilance, Rao Maldeo bestowed the messenger with precious alms and jewels and urgently assembled his brave comrades to proceed towards Ajmer. It was the January of 1544 CE. The Rathore army was setting up camp in Giri, whereas their enemies were pitched at Sumel.[11]

Initially, both sides were reluctant to fight. Rao Maldeo's chieftains considered retreating from Giri but were convinced otherwise by Rao Pichyaansiji, Rao Jaitji and Rao Kumpaji, amongst others. They reminded their hesitant chieftains that the land upon which they stood belonged to their ancestors. As Rathores, it was their duty and birthright to protect their motherland with their life.

Simultaneously, Sher Shah Suri felt dread creeping up on him after he laid eyes on Rao Maldeo's militia. Just when Suri was considering changing his mind and stepping back, Rao Veeramdevji pacified him with a ploy that would make his brother's defeat certain.[12] He assured Sher Shah Suri that his older brother could be vanquished not with the sword but with the mind, that is, using deceit and trickery.[13]

Rao Maldeo's selfishness had maligned his younger brother over the years, who would soon use his familiarity to his advantage. Rao Veeramdevji hatched a plan to obtain one lakh gold coins, which he then sent to the Rathore camp in Giri, some 8 miles away, with the offer of a subsidized exchange rate. Next, he ordered Sher Shah Suri's secretaries to write royal orders of allegiance inside a hundred sewn shields. These, too, were to be traded in a similar fashion.

Once Rao Veeramdevji's plotted transaction was over, he wrote a secret letter to his brother that read, 'Your illegitimate acquisition of Merta forced me to seek the mighty Sher Shah Suri's shelter. But I wonder why all of your men have pledged their loyalty to Sher Shah. To prove this allegation, I must inform you that your warriors have accepted Sher Shah's coinage. You may also tear apart the cushions in their shields to confirm this treachery of theirs.'

Mortified by the acerbic letter, Rao Maldeo sent his detectives to investigate his brother's charges and was stupefied to receive their nod in confirmation. This traumatic revelation and its sense of betrayal kept the Rathore king from sleeping that night. When his loyalists arrived to greet him the following morning, he scrutinized their shields to discover that his brother was right. They contained a royal decree by Sher Shah Suri that read, 'Kindly expedite the fulfilment of your promise to arrest Rao Maldeo and surrender him to me. I write this degree with my personal pledge to judiciously divide Marwar amongst you all and to ensure your steady progress. Each one of you will receive a tip of one thousand coins, provided you execute the task without further delay'.[14]

Rao Maldeo was left shell-shocked by the alleged treachery of his soldiers. He felt the ground slipping beneath his feet. Albeit unethically, Rao Veeramdevji had strategically triumphed over his older brother. Turning a deaf ear to the endless persuasion by his people, a morally defeated Rao Maldeo began to retreat to Jodhpur. However, Rao Maldeo's men grew so resentful of Rao Veeramdevji's foul play that they unanimously vowed to defend their motherland from Sher Shah Suri and his allies. As part of this pledge, Rao Kumpaji, Rao Jaitji and Rao Pichyaansiji unflinchingly galloped into a bloodbath, knowing they had no chance of surviving. While the Rajputs barely added up to 12,000, Sher Shah Suri's army of 1,20,000 Afghans was tenfold in comparison. At this juncture, even though Suri's victory was imminent, the mighty Rathores lacked the slightest ounce of fear. Each one went down fighting and slayed Sher Shah Suri's men.

Even after they emerged victorious, Sher Shah Suri and his men praised the unsurpassable Rathore fortitude. Sher Shah said, 'Thank god for this (victory), else I would have lost my stronghold over Hindustan for the sake of a fistful of millets.'[15] As a consequence of the tragic war at Giri-Sumel, Sher Shah Suri took possession of Jodhpur as well as the entire stretch from Ajmer to Mount Abu. As shall be discovered over the following chapter, Rao Maldeo would take another year to reclaim his motherland from Sher Shah Suri's clutches.[16]

3

Rao Maheshdasji

A Loyal Ally

The palanquin from Dewaliya carried a Sisodia princess, Umed Kanwar, to Kheenvsar after her wedding to Rao Pichyaansiji. Soon after, she birthed his royal heir, Rao Maheshdasji.[1] His father's ceaseless military participation in faraway lands called for Rao Maheshdasji to prematurely attain knowledge of politics and governance. When Rao Pichyaansiji was executed by Sher Shah Suri's army, Kheenvsar was left in the agile hands of his son.

Blood before Water

At the time, many of his cousins had withdrawn military support from Jodhpur to pursue their own sovereign interests. Unlike them, Rao Maheshdasji had pledged Kheenvsar's unabated substantiation to Marwar's forces during the reign of Rao Gangaji and his son, Rao Maldeo. The unbroken ties of loyalty upheld by the Karamsots towards Marwar seem to have misled several imprudent historians, who have erroneously chronicled Kheenvsar as a subsidiary of Jodhpur. As we shall soon discover, this conjecture gradually evolved into a historical misapprehension with adverse consequences.

Contrary to these erroneous claims, Rao Jodhaji had consolidated Marwar's stronghold by encouraging his sons to expand their kingdom in the form of sovereign republics of their own. Rao Maldeo impounded the autonomy of several Rathore states and unwarrantedly revoked Rao Jodhaji's will. In Kheenvsar's case, Rao Maheshdasji spent his entire life in subservience until his final years, when Kheenvsar's autonomy was granted back to him. Even in the face of this grave unjustness, Rao Maheshdasji extended unconditional support to Rao Maldeo.

A Reclamation of the Motherland

It wasn't long after facing defeat in Giri-Sumel that the obdurate Rathore army revived itself for another encounter with Sher Shah Suri. Sher Shah had resumed his territorial expansion after leaving Marwar under the charge of 5,000 cadets in Bhagesar.[2] In 1545 CE, news of his death in Kalinjar reached Jodhpur.[3] Rao Maldeo seized this opportunity to assemble his forces and clobber the Bhagesar ranks. The time had arrived for him to end Sher Shah Suri's 524-day-long siege of Marwar.[4] Rao Maheshdasji was also present in this redemptive quest.

After a successful campaign in Bhagesar, Rao Maldeo's spirits soared high. In shared enthusiasm, his men succeeded in capturing Jaisalmer from the Bhatis. What followed was a hat-trick attempt against his cousin, Rao Jaimal, in Merta. A hesitant Rao Maheshdasji was compelled to attack someone he considered his own for the sake of supreme command.[5] Much to Rao Maldeo's astonishment, Rao Jaimal's troops persisted in their defence of Merta. The Marwar army eventually relented, thereby forcing Rao Maldeo to return disappointed to Jodhpur.

The Merta Offensive

During a skirmish with Rana Uday Singh's Mewar army, Ajmer's Haji Khan Pathan sought Rao Maldeo's intervention. The latter obliged by endorsing the Pathan ruler with some of his bravest chieftains and a mighty cavalry of 1,500. He was camping in Jaitaran when Rao Maldeo received news of Haji Khan's victory. Cognizant that Merta had lost Mewar as an ally due to Pathan's recent conquest, Rao Maldeo made another advance towards Merta. As he had schemed, Marwar succeeded this time, and a thwarted Rao Jaimal vanished into the thick crevices of Mewar.

Rao Maldeo celebrated his newest territorial conquest by adorning it with the Malkot Fort. Relegating Merta as a vassal of Jodhpur under Rao Maheshdasji's supervision, he made his way home to resume his kingly duties. In time, Rao Jaimal was reinstated in Merta with the support of the illustrious Mughal emperor, Akbar. Rao Maldeo retaliated by dispatching the army of his son, Yuvraj Chandrasen, to join Rao Maheshdasji and Merta's loyal guardians. Consequentially, Akbar's army attacked Merta from both sides. Rao Maheshdasji and his compatriots died defending Merta against the Mughal army, which trampled over them to gain control over Merta and its neighbouring provinces.[6]

Shortly before Rao Maheshdasji's demise in Merta, Marwar restored him autonomy over Kheenvsar.[7]

Contradictorily, a majority of historical archives confirm that the sirayat system was first introduced during the governance of Sawai Raja Sur Singhji, who was born almost a century and a half after Rao Maldeo's demise.[8] As per this claim, it is highly unlikely that Kheenvsar faced a demotion from its sirayat rank any time before 1617.

Karamsot Echoes of Sacrifice

The martyrdom of Kheenvsar's first three scions in Marwar's military conquests bears testament to the unflinching loyalty of the Karamsots. The fourth Karamsot ruler, Thakur Hardasji, came of age in the relative absence of his father. He grew up under the watchful eyes of Rao Maheshdasji's foresighted consorts, under whose guidance Rao Hardasji grew increasingly conscious of his kingly duties. His selfless forefathers had sacrificed their interests for Marwar's sovereignty. Kheenvsar and its people wistfully longed for their king. Perhaps one day, his son would come to their aid.

4

Thakur Hardasji

The Righteous Guardian

A prime inspiration for Rao Hardasji as he grew up was his father's Shekhawat queen from Kalyanpur.

Immortalized as Padam Kanwar, she remains etched in Kheenvsar's history in the form of Padamsar, a water reservoir she commissioned for her beloved people.[1]

As per a handwritten archive, Thakur Hardasji was accorded the jagir of a village named Khariya.[2] Meanwhile, Kheenvsar was retained by Marwar as a satellite state since the martyrdom of Rao Maheshdasji in 1562 until 1617. In 1617, Sawai Raja Sur Singhji returned Kheenvsar to Thakur Hardasji to felicitate his bravery. By then, Kheenvsar's Thakur had grown old and had spent most of his life deprived of his sovereign motherland. The time between 1562 and 1617 seems precarious for Kheenvsar in that its custodianship was obscure. That said, some historical sources argue that the sirayat system was established by Rao Maldeo and was later officiated by Sawai Raja Sur Singhji.[3]

The declassification of his royal title and the delayed recognition of Thakur Hardasji's sovereignty over Kheenvsar were later revealed to be deliberate stratagems. Rao Maldeo had violated the Rathore tradition of primogeniture when he appointed his third son, Rao Chandrasen, as his successor. The newly-appointed Rao refused to oblige his cousin Jaitmal in revoking the death penalty accorded to one of his slaves.[4] His refusal to grant the hapless slave a life sentence and his inhumane order to have him killed earned Rao Chandrasen the ill will of many Rathores.

Meanwhile, Rao Maldeo's eldest son, who is referred to as Mota Raja Udai Singh, felt betrayed by the coronation of his younger brother and launched a series of feuds against him. Thakur Hardasji was amongst those who emerged in outright support of Mota Raja Udai Singh's right to the throne by virtue of primogeniture. Thus, Kheenvsar's new allegiance attracted Rao Chandrasen's rancour and distrust. Notwithstanding the ruler's disfavour, Thakur Hardasji presided over Kheenvsar with the same regard and goodwill as his predecessors.

A Feud for the Throne

Soon, the acrimony between Rao Chandrasen and his older brother reached a boiling point in Lohawat, where they clashed in a feud over the throne. Even though Mota Raja Udai Singh captured Gangani and Bawdi from Rao Chandrasen, he was gravely injured by Chandrasen's chieftain Meghraj and was compelled to accept defeat.[5] Thakur Hardasji and his younger brother, Kalyandasji, had defended Mota Raja Udai Singh with their sweat and blood, and Kalyandasji perished on the battlefield.

In a bard in Saubhagya Singh Shekhawat's compilation, *Rajasthani Veer Geet*, Thakur Hardasji is mentioned as the *jagirdaar* of Daawra.[6] This indicates a likelihood of him being awarded multiple jagirs from Jodhpur.

Mughal Alliance in Ahmedabad

Jodhpur's throne was eventually occupied by Mota Raja Udai Singh, who was succeeded by his son, Sawai Raja Sur Singhji. Thakur Hardasji had lent his arduous support to the father–son duo and departed for the upcoming military advance in Ahmedabad. The new king, Sawai Raja Sur Singhji, received orders from Mughal emperor Akbar to tackle the defiant Bahadur Khan in Gujarat. Bahadur Khan was a sultan of the Muzaffarid dynasty who ascended the throne after overthrowing his brothers.[7] His unscrupulous means of attaining power had earned him much Mughal contempt. In 1572, Thakur Hardasji accompanied Sawai Raja Sur Singhji's army to Ahmedabad and valiantly fought against the Muzaffarid sultan. This battle was significant in Indian history because it released Gujarat from the clutches of the Muzaffarids after two centuries and annexed it under the Mughal Empire.

A Revision of the Rathore Durbar

In 1595 CE, Sawai Raja Sur Singhji's prime minister, Govind Das Bhati, decidedly altered the traditional format of the Rathore durbar to closely resemble Mughal protocols. As per the revised system, a designated seating order was introduced for the royal *deewans, bakshis, karkhaan daftaris, darogas, hakims* and other important state officials.

Ever since Rao Jodha's time, royal protocol called for all of his 24 brothers to be towards the left side of the throne, thereby gaining the denomination of *daavi misal* or the left precedence. Concomitantly, the 17 *Jodhawats* (sons of Jodha) occupied the right side of the throne as the durbar's *jeevni misal* or right precedence. Barring this segregation, there was no officiating rank or order in place, and the Rathore durbar believed that mutual ties of brotherhood overrode all provincial hierarchies.

This format was radically altered and reorganized by Prime Minister Bhati, who classified Marwar's eight prime jagirs to paramountcy as sirayats. These included Aasop, Auwa, Bagdi, Kanana, Khairwa, Raipur, Riya and Kheenvsar. Sirayats are principalities that were accorded the *sire ka kurab*, an exalted rank that loosely corresponds with the cabinet rank in the Maharaja's durbar. Given their recently elevated status, the rulers of these eight principalities were seated right after the Maharaja and his immediate family. An upgradation over their contemporaries notwithstanding, the sirayats remained under Marwar's supremacy. These erstwhile sovereign provinces had upheld an undying loyalty towards the Jodhpur durbar, but by means of an ordinance, they were reduced to mere satellite states. Their autonomy was now overshadowed by a total and indefinite eclipse.

The Bhati Assassinations

History notes Prime Minister Govind Das Bhati's corrupt usurpations of power. In one such instance, Mota Raja Udai Singhji's younger son, Kishan Singhji, had been proclaimed his successor.[8] This decision had echoed even in the Mughal courts, but Bhati dared to prevent Kishan Singhji from occupying his father's seat. Sur Singhji was crowned instead, and the area of Roopnagar was given to Kishan Singhji as consolation. He cultivated it under his guardianship as Kishangarh.

After spending a few years in indignation, Kishan Singhji vented his hatred towards the miscreant prime minister in 1615 CE. Kishan Singhji unleashed an attack on Govind Das Bhati's brother, Surtan Singh, in Merta. Thakur Hardasji received this news, and no sooner had he reached the site to restrain Kishan Singhji than Surtan Singh was killed.

In a retributive effort, Prime Minister Govind Das Bhati mobilized Yuvraj Gaj Singh I's army and the two set out for Merta. Upon reaching Merta, they found that the prime assassin of the feud, Gopal Das Rathore, had departed for Kharkhari to tend to his injuries. Joined by Thakur Hardasji, Yuvraj Gaj Singh I and his prime minister soon caught up with the killer and annihilated him.[9]

During his visit to Ajmer in 1615 CE, Mughal Emperor Jahangir met Sawai Raja Sur Singhji, Yuvraj Gaj Singh I, Govind Das Bhati and Thakur Hardas Singhji. Kishan Singhji, too, had arrived from his neighbouring abode of Kishangarh to solicit the emperor's permission to ambush Govind Das Bhati's camp in the thick of the night. Thus, through foul play, Kishan Singhji took revenge against the Bhatis. This foul play on Kishan Singhji's part wouldn't be ignored by Sawai Raja Sur Singhji, who sent his young prince, Yuvraj Gaj Singh I, with Thakur Hardasji and other loyalists to eliminate the culprit. In the end, justice was served for the slain Bhati brothers, with Kishan Singhji being laid to eternal rest.[10]

Thakur Hardasji was celebrated in numerous ballads for his trustworthiness, valour and grit. One amongst these praises him generously and even equates his integrity with Lord Brahma, yogic wisdom with Lord Shiva and his worth with the 14 gems of the ocean.[11] Thakur Hardasji also left his mark with his charitable nature, which Sohan Singh Dholirao evokes as follows[12]:

> Rao Hardasji Nava likhaay ghoro pich deeno kada dina poshaak siropaav dina 111 rupaye kaldar chaandi ke diye. Kheenvsar su sthaan samat 1645 mein Rao Fatehdan ne.

When translated, it means that the immensely generous Rao Hardasji showered all with his bounties and gifts. In 1645, he presented Rao Fatehdan with five kalyaan horses, costumes and dresses, amulets and a donation of 111 rupees.[13]

Rao Hardasji's monarchical fire was soon rekindled by a son borne by his first wife, Thakurani Kehar Kanwar, a Chauhan princess from Chhota Udaipur.[14] Their scion would go down in Kheenvsar's history as its fifth luminary, Thakur Dayaldasji.

5

Thakur Dayaldasji

The Itinerant King

The fifth Karamsot inheritor, Thakur Dayaldasji, was a thorough loyalist of the then Mughal Emperor Shah Jahan and is said to have served him over a prolonged period in the Mughal capital of Agra. His inexorable service towards the Mughal crown accorded him several jagirs between Kekdi and Fuliya, but alas, Shah Jahan's inclination towards Thakur Dayaldasji soon took a back seat for an error that the Karamsot noble didn't commit. The Mughal *badshah* had sanctioned Bikaner's Maharaja Dalpat Singhji a homeward trip only after Kheenvsar's *thakur* agreed to serve as the guarantor of his timely return. When the desert sands gave no signs of the Maharaja's return, Shah Jahan penalized Maharaja Dalpat Singhji by suspending his ranking, and Thakur Dayaldasji, too, followed suit as the unsuccessful guarantor.[1]

When Thakur Dayaldasji reached Kheenvsar, his spirits fell further. The then king of Jodhpur, Maharaja Jaswant Singhji I, had confiscated Kheenvsar's autonomy and transferred it to the thakur's cousin, Prithviraj. To endure the treatment rendered to an outcast in his own home was painful. Thakur Dayaldasji rejected the idea of becoming subservient to his usurping cousin and wasted no time in stepping away from this mockery. He made way for Mundel, a village he had won by trouncing its reigning Solankis. This hamlet flourished under Thakur Dayaldasji's capable guardianship and gradually came to be known as Madpura.

Shortly after his relocation, he built his palace and a temple dedicated to the Rathore kuldevi, Nagnechya Mataji. However, before he could fully reap the fruits of his resettlement, he lost one of his beloved queens, Princess Aas Kanwar Bhati of Bikampur. As her name suggests, she was pined for by her widowed king. One day, he found that the bowl of his staple yoghurt was missing from his *thaali*. 'If only my bygone queen was alive today, none of my best interests would stand ignored,' he lamented. Shortly after uttering these words, the bereaved thakur had an epiphany. Perhaps he could preserve the worldly presence of his queen by asking her father for his younger daughter's hand. His wish was granted. However, the young queen agreed to marry him on one condition: he would grant Madpura's sole succession to their son. Thakur Dayaldasji obliged, but as fate would have it, an urgent commitment arose in the form of a watermelon. The thakur had to depart at once, relegating his queen and their newborn son to uncertainty.

Mateere ki Raad

Even after all these centuries, today, citizens of Nagaur and Bikaner retell stories of the dreadful battle that ensued over a watermelon sprout. A seed in Nagaur's peripheral village of Jakhaniya unknowingly sprouted across the invisible border from the adjoining soils of Bikaner's Siwana village. The two princely states shared an arbitrary border between these villages, and when a farmer from Siwana harvested the fruit, a proprietorial outrage broke out amongst the farmers on both sides. This seemingly petty quarrel soon became the prime cause of a strife between the two states. Nagaur's Rao Amar Singhji and Bikaner's Maharaja Karan Singhji were now at loggerheads, and Kheenvsar was called upon to douse the fire.

When the dispute took place, both the kings were at Shah Jahan's court in Agra. The two pleaded to be dispersed by Shah Jahan to tend to affairs pertaining to their respective kingdoms, but the Mughal emperor made a biased verdict. When he sensed the severity of the situation, he permitted Maharaja Karan Singhji to defend Bikaner but retained Rao Amar Singhji in his court. The subsequent return of their ruler allowed Bikaner to mobilize a mighty army of over 4,000. Across the border, Thakur Dayaldasji and Rao Amar Singhji's minister, Seehmal Singhvi, commanded 3,000 soldiers to represent Nagaur's remotely situated king.[2]

The placid day of 9 October 1642 was jolted by a heated confrontation between the two armies. Mankind's pettiness over an unsuspecting watermelon made a ghastly appearance. The carnage that claimed hundreds of lives on either side ended with Bikaner emerging as the victor. Three arrows and a sword struck Thakur Dayaldasji before he admitted defeat. Although he survived, his second son, Kunwar Bhagwandas, perished on the battleground. His bravery continues to be honoured by the people of Gura, the village he founded.

The Itinerant Princes

Thakur Dayaldas was a liberal-minded king who wasn't dismayed by his failure to retrieve Kheenvsar. He bore lofty dreams of developing and expanding the Karamsot capital but decided against discord. He embarked upon his heavenly journey sometime after the Nagaur–Bikaner war.

Thakur Bhim Singhji, who was the first in line for succession, fulfilled the late thakur's promise by granting Madpura to his younger half-brother, Kesri Singh. Meanwhile, he migrated towards Devina Kumari ki Dhaani in 1651 and made provisions for what presently stands as the village of Deu. The sixth Karamsot was birthed with a predestination vastly different from his father's. The time had arrived for Kheenvsar's itinerant prince to reclaim his ancestral land.

6

Thakur Bhim Singhji

The Restorer of Glory

Rarely does the world encounter morally upright rulers who choose to uphold their principles and values at the cost of self-effacement. Thakur Bhim Singhji is inscribed in the annals of Rajputana as a man of his word. *Praan jaaye par vachan na jaye* is a well-known Indian proverb that denotes the primary virtue of staying true to one's word, even if that entails giving up one's life. A slightly altered version that substitutes *vachan* with *shaan* (pride) rhymes as well and has persisted over the centuries. By fulfilling his half-brother's inheritance of Madpura, Thakur Bhim Singhji not only upheld his father's commitment and honour but also chose filial trusteeship over self-interest. By virtue of primogeniture, he could have retained his sovereignty over Madpura, but he accorded it as per his father's wishes. Executing his father's promise threw the young thakur's future into some amount of uncertainty, but righteousness is deterred by nothing. As we will soon discover, karma had its part to play.

Border Loots

As is evident in the previous chapter, Marwar's Maharaja Jaswant Singhji I particularly favoured Thakur Dayaldasji's cousin brother, Prithvirajji, and transferred Kheenvsar's reigns into his hands.

When the Maharaja was away in Delhi, his kingdom's growth had begun to plateau. The royal treasurers reported that recurring pillages on the border were the prime contributors to the recent stagnation of Marwar's economic growth. The most notorious amongst these pillagers was the then chieftain of Bikampur, Thakur Balu Singh Bhati. News of these pillages swiftly found their way to Maharaja Jaswant Singhji I, who turned to Prithvirajji to intervene. The latter was given supreme orders to curb these exploitations with immediate effect. Because Bikampur was Thakur Bhim

Singhji's maternal home, a resolution of any kind was improbable without his mediation. Prithvirajji was also anxious that his plan might be sabotaged if Balu Singh Bhati caught even the faintest hint of the operation. To proceed with the matter, he sent for Thakur Bhim Singhji and informed him of the Maharaja's diktat.

Perceiving it as a matter that purely served the interests of Maharaja Jaswant Singh I, Thakur Bhim Singhji repudiated the proposal and asked what was in it for him. In a desperate bid to appease the Maharaja, Prithvirajji swore to his cousin that if they succeeded, he would step down from his seat and return Kheenvsar to Thakur Bhim Singhji.

Pleased with this arrangement, he shook hands with Prithvirajji, and his involvement assured Marwar's victory over the looters. So thrilled was Prithvirajji over his success that he marched to Delhi carrying the decapitated head of Thakur Balu Singh Bhati to present at the Maharaja's feet. The king expressed his appreciation for Prithvirajji, rewarded him the jagir of Peepad and graced the promise made to Thakur Bhim Singhji by reinstating him on Kheenvsar's royal seat. The year was 1648 when the sixth direct descendant of Kheenvsar's Karamsot Rathore returned home. He was welcomed by his people, who showered him with flowers and uttered slogans to praise his glory. Indeed, Kheenvsar's custodian had made a jubilant return, and justice had finally been delivered.

Mughal Wars of Succession

In his first war of succession, Mughal prince Aurangzeb fiercely clashed against Maharaja Jaswant Singhji I, who had allied with Aurangzeb's older brother and the rightful Mughal heir, Dara Shikoh. Marwar's Maharaja mobilized his troops towards Malwa and battled the Mughals in the neighbouring area of Dharmat. Thakur Bhim Singhji was among the chieftains who led Marwar's military advance for Dara Shikoh.

Due to their superior artillery and war tactics, Aurangzeb's side emerged victorious. No sooner had the victors turned towards Agra than Dara Shikoh, along with the Rathores, ambushed them in Fatehbad. Aurangzeb and his other brother, Murad Baksh, retaliated with heavy cannon fire. Murad Baksh's bow struck Rajput leader Raja Rautela headlong, and the Rathore army was rendered leaderless. Alarmed, Dara Shikoh began to descend his *howdah,* only to be deserted by his elephant. The remaining Rajput contenders perceived this as a sign of defeat and yielded to Aurangzeb, henceforth swearing their allegiance to him.

Defending Marwar's flag, Thakur Bhim Singhji wasn't the sole son of Kheenvsar during the Dharmat and Fatehbad combats.[1] His fury was restrained, in part, by his two princes, Kunwar Hari Singhji and Kunwar Harnath Singhji, who were only teenagers back then.

The Sixth Afghan–Mughal War (1668–1669)

The young Karamsot scions had served their Maharaja for five long years during his deputation against Sujan Khan in the valleys of Peshawar.[2]

Amidst the Mughal wars of succession, several Afghan tribes in the northwestern frontiers seized the opportunity to raid Mughal districts in Peshawar. In 1671 CE the

Mughals stationed Jodhpur's Maharaja Jaswant Singhji I at Jamrud to suppress any further Afghan incursions.

During his military deputation, the Maharaja was accompanied by several Rajput clansmen. One of them was Thakur Bhim Singhji's older son, Thakur Hari Singhji. In 1669, he and 49 brave Rajput warriors met their end alongside Maharaja Jaswant Singhji I during the Sixth Afghan–Mughal War. Hundreds of miles away from their motherland, in the foreign soils of Peshawar, the brave Rathore contingent was the sole defending force beneath the Khyber Pass before being wiped out by the Yousufzai Pathans.

Kunwar Hari Singhji's legacy prevailed in the *thikanas* of Achina and Tantawas, and his younger brother succeeded the Karamsot dynasty as Thakur Harnath Singhji. Their younger brothers, Gopinathji and Fateh Singhji, inherited Aakla and Deu, respectively. Chattar Singhji, the fifth son of Thakur Bhim Singhji, was childless. There are mentions of Thakur Bhim Singhji's chhatris being erected anterior to Kheenvsar Fort's main gate. Whether this claim is true is unclear due to Aurangzeb's brutal maiming of Kheenvsar's multiple relics.

7
Thakur Harnath Singhji
The Heroic Martyr

Having lost his older brother to the Afghans in Jamrud, Thakur Harnath Singhji undertook his imperial duties by virtue of being Thakur Bhim Singh's oldest surviving son. The seventh Karamsot chief had steadfastly supported his father and older brother in the war expeditions that claimed both their lives.

Guardians of Marwar

Eleven years before Maharaja Jaswant Singhji I's death, his first and only son, Yuvraj Prithvirajji, had succumbed to Aurangzeb's betrayal, wherein the Mughal Emperor had presented him with a poisoned *khilat.* The tragic and untimely death of his only son had shattered the Maharaja beyond recovery. A decade later, his martyrdom in Peshawar rendered Marwar heirless and in pandemonium, but a silver lining soon emerged. Two of the deceased king's queens, who had accompanied him to Lahore, discovered that they were pregnant. Of the two newborns, only one, Ajit Singhji, survived, and it was upon his embryonic state that the future of Marwar decidedly rested. The infant was fated to be Jodhpur's Maharaja by birth.

Still unaware of the royal infant, Aurangzeb began blatantly meddling with Marwar's internal affairs. Given its vulnerable state of affairs, he threw his licentious gaze upon the kingless empire. He imposed Muslim rule and accelerated a swift Mughal annexation of Marwar. He ordered Hindu practices to be suppressed and the Hindu populace to be forcibly converted to Islam. Under Aurangzeb's religious fundamentalism, several Hindu temples were plundered, women raped, idols maimed and relics destroyed. Dark times had befallen Marwar, and terror engulfed it from all sides.

When Aurangzeb received news of the late Maharaja's

infant, he refused to recognize Ajit Singhji as the new Maharaja. Instead, he placed Marwar under the titular regency of a chieftain named Indra Singh and proceeded to attend to more pressing issues in Delhi.

The legendary Rathore warrior, Veer Durgadasji, rushed to Delhi with Sonagji Champawat, Thakur Harnath Singhji and other Rathores to challenge Aurangzeb's appointment of a regent. Various Mughal attacks inflected them on their way, which they overcame and reached the Mughal Emperor. They asserted Maharaja Ajit Singhji's legitimacy as Marwar's successor and pledged to guard the infant's empire until he came of age. Aurangzeb turned down the proposition and offered a title and grant to Maharaja Ajit Singhji on the condition that he be raised in the imperial harem in the presence of his queen mothers.

Upon further negotiation, Aurangzeb agreed to return Jodhpur's throne to the infant king, provided that he was raised in the Muslim faith. These unscrupulous propositions outraged the Rajput cohort, and Veer Durgadasji waged a 30-year-long battle against the Mughals after escaping with the newborn king. On 25 June 1679, Maharaja Ajit Singhji's nurse, Goora Dhaa, placed her own son upon the royal bed and secretly handed over the sleeping king to Veer Durgadasji in a basket. Strapping Maharaja Ajit Singhji to his back, Veer Durgadasji galloped to Jodhpur atop his stallion, Arbudh. His compatriots left no stone unturned in providing him cover and countered Mughal retaliations until the latter eventually tired and gave in to the unrelenting Rathores and Sisodias.[1]

Durgadas Rathore mounting his stallion;
Courtesy of Mehrangarh Museum Trust

This scheme was undoubtedly perilous, but the brave Rathores were prepared to go to any extent to rescue Marwar from Aurangzeb's tyrannical grasp. Including Veer Durgadasji, bards narrate that only four out of four hundred warriors survived this mission. Thus, from 1679 to Aurangzeb's death in 1707, the first and only foreign invasion occurred in Jodhpur's history. Maharaja Ajit Singhji had been safely carried back to Jodhpur, but a long road still lay ahead of Marwar. The enormous possibility of the infant Maharaja being endangered by Mughal cunningness weighed heavily upon the Rathores. To ward off any such possibilities, Veer Durgadasji entrusted Maharaja Ajit Singhji's upbringing in the hands of Jugji Purohit in Kalandri, a village in Sirohi. Here, in the unsuspecting fringes of southern Marwar, the anticipated monarch was anonymously raised.

Until Maharaja Ajit Singhji grew up to assume supreme power, Veer Durgadasji, Sonagji Champawat and Thakur Harnath Singhji didn't sleep a peaceful wink, for uncertainty loomed large upon a Marwar that longed for its king to return.

The Rathores vs Aurangzeb

In the year after Veer Durgadasji's abduction of Maharaja Ajit Singhji, Aurangzeb sent his son, Prince Akbar, in another bid to suppress the Rajput army. Upon reaching Sojat, he was met with a variety of anti-Mughal rallies led by the Rajputs. Having borne heavy losses in Delhi, Veer Durgadasji considered it wise to substitute an armed resistance with diplomatic talks to win the Mughal prince in their favour. Negotiations commenced with Prince Akbar, who was visited by many Rathores, including Thakur Harnathji. They succeeded in persuading the Mughal prince, and reports of this conspiracy made Aurangzeb belligerent. He launched his troops against his rebelling son, who fled towards the Deccan with Veer Durgadasji's assistance. Prince Akbar sought Maratha asylum under Sambhaji Bhosale, while Aurangzeb's militia fought Marwar's Rajputs in numerous encounters at Bhardrajun, Phalaudi, Sojat and Pali. Amongst the defending combatants, Thakur Harnathji protected the Rathore stronghold at Ustra, where he grappled with Anop Singh Kumpawat, a Rajput who had switched sides and joined Aurangzeb. The Karamsot king firmly held onto Ustra, even though it cost him the agony of numerous Mughal assaults.

The Jalore Conspiracy

Maharaja Ajit Singhji had grown into a tactful ruler and wielded immense leverage in Mughal politics. When he acquired Aurangzeb's nod to reside in Jalore, many of his chieftains felt displeased and sought the intervention of Nagaur's Mohkam Singhji. Together, they hatched a ploy to capture the Maharaja, who they believed was turning into a Mughal sympathizer. Thakur Harnathji promptly departed to safeguard his king from the Nagaur rebellion, which took place by the name of the Battle of Raythal Dhuneda.

Many of the Maharaja's bravehearts endured bullets and arrows, and only a handful of them lived on to celebrate the king's return to Jodhpur following Aurangzeb's death in 1707. Finally, Marwar's king had returned, and three arduous decades of their king's absence had ended. Maharaja Ajit Singhji felicitated each one of Marwar's champions for their unyielding devotion throughout the years. He knew that without these sentinels, neither his survival nor his return would have been possible.

He also saluted Karamsot bravado and expressed gratitude towards Kheenvsar for its unrelieved participation in Marwar's preservation. Thakur Harnath Singhji hadn't been Kheenvsar's sole representative in Maharaja Ajit Singhji's liberation army. In fact, many of his brothers, sons, cousins and nephews took up arms to protect their king.

Thakur Harnath Singhji was granted his ancestral sovereignty over Kheenvsar as a token of the Maharaja's gratitude. His Karamsot brethren were awarded several jagirs of Marwar. Lieutenant-Colonel James Tod also records a visit the Maharaja paid to his brethren in Kheenvsar, where he was received with much pomp and splendour. Seven generations and counting, the Karamsots proved their unwavering allegiance to Jodhpur time and again and were repeatedly acknowledged as amongst Marwar's foremost custodians.

The Sambar War

Aurangzeb's obsession for Rajputana was inherited by his successor, Bahadur Shah I, who led a vast Mughal army towards Amer and annexed it without a battle, forcing Sawai Jai Singhji to retreat. He shrewdly took advantage of a familial dispute and appointed the Sawai's younger brother, Vijai Singh, to rule over Amer as Mirza Raja. The Mughals hoisted their flag atop Amer Fort and renamed Amer to Mominabad. Bahadur Shah I's quest for Amer was mirrored in Jodhpur, where a separate battalion sought to overthrow Maharaja Ajit Singhji.

Both the subjugated Rajput kings, Sawai Jai Singhji and Maharaja Ajit Singhji, ushered their armies under the commandership of Veer Durgadasji. Their armies were ordered to converge at a mid-point in Pushkar, from where they planned a united foray against Bahadur Shah I. The then subedar of Ajmer, Sujat Khan, persuaded the kings to pause in Pushkar with the shrewd intention of buying time to send word to the Mughal emperor. Sujat Khan further cajoled the Sawai and Maharaja by promising that he would have their ranks officiated by the Mughal Badshah. In the meantime, Bahadur Shah I was alerted, and he made a brisk military advent towards

Pushkar. Caught unawares, the Rajputs were cannoned by the Mughals.

In the initial phase, the battle favoured the Mughal offensive, led by Mewat's subedar, Syed Hussain Khan, alongside the military officers of Merta and Narnaul. No sooner had they become overconfident about their perceived victory than the Rajput armies temporarily backtracked behind a hillock. Assuming that the Rajput armies had deserted the battlefield, several Mughal soldiers began looting Rajput supplies. Just then, the Rajputs made a recalibrated surprise attack via their alternate battalion, which was kept hidden from the enemy camp.

The Rajput camel cavalry cruised across the war grounds, stupefying Bahadur Shah I's allies before beheading Hussain Khan and his likes. Thakur Harnath Singhji charged into the thick of the fray and went down fighting one of the Mughal commanders. His heroic feat in this battle inspired several tributes from distinguished poets and historians. Sandhu Kumbhakaran's verses were later reproduced by Jodhpur's famous historian, Pandit Ramkarna Asopa, in 1928 via a handwritten note. Their collective praises can vaguely be translated as follows:

Blessed and brave is he, who,
astride his lightning-fast yellow horse,
pierces the opposing army to slash his enemies
and strangle them with his powerful arms,
who thumps against their mighty elephants
with the single-handed use of his lustrous shield.
The brave king of Karamsots slays endless invaders,
whose corpses form a mushy pile of

rusting blood that his horse stomps over,
pulverizing them under their hoofs.
He fought against one after the other
until he could fight no more.
His loyal horse took a fine beating
and down they went in unison.
But before he did, it was him (Thakur Harnath Singhji)
who superseded Delhi's unit of the Mughal army.
And like a wasp whizzing past the war grounds,
lethally stinging anyone who dared to stop him.
He bathed in the blood of five Mughal commanders
before rejoicing in the heavens above.

As any bilingual mind can ascertain, much meaning is lost in translation, and these verses are but a faint replication of what the gifted poets and historians had originally penned down. Nevertheless, this translation offers valuable insight into the sheer ferocity that earned Thakur Harnath Singhji these posthumous tributes, given freely and without any expectation of acclaim or propaganda.

Two of Thakur Harnath Singhji's five queens, namely, Thakurani Hans Kanwar Chauhan and Thakurani Abhay Kanwar Bhati, are recorded to have performed sati in Kheenvsar. Their divine legacy remains etched in Kheenvsar today in the form of Thakur Harnath Singhji's chhatri and the Sati Matas' hand imprints that were later engraved in stone.

Sati Pol, Kheenvsar

8
Thakur Udai Singhji
The Fearless Warrior

Thakur Harnath Singhji bequeathed Kheenvsar to his eldest son, Thakur Udai Singhji. Reigning for 21 years, he ensured Marwar's buoyancy over the placid waters of Kheenvsar.

The Regal Intermarriages

In 1719, Mehrangarh made a grand display to welcome Marwar's new son-in-law, Jaipur's Sawai Jai Singhji. The royal procession had graced Marwar to seek the hand of its daughter, and distinguished nobles and chieftains rejoiced in this alliance, savouring the sweetness of jaggery as a symbol of celebration. Baijilal Suraj Kanwar of Marwar was carried in a heavenly palanquin to the Kachhwaha capital of Jaipur as its queen.

Maharaja Ajit Singhji breathed his last in 1724. His firstborn and Marwar's new monarch, Maharaja Abhay Singhji, was in Delhi to recover the administrative units the Mughals had seized from his father, namely, Nagaur, Kekdi, Ghatiyali, Mareth, Parbatsar and Fuliya. His sovereign powers over Marwar had gained Mughal validation.

While the Maharaja was in Delhi, he received a marriage proposal from the same royal house that his sister was married into. It took his chieftains little time upon receiving his consent, to begin the wedding preparations. However, they took offence when Maharaja Abhay Singhji opted for his marital ceremonies to be held in Mathura. After resisting voracious bouts of persuasion from his clansmen, the Maharaja's wishes were granted and he was wedded to the princess of Jaipur in the sacred birthplace of Lord Krishna. Many of his fellow men handled their disappointment by deserting the wedding procession and returning home.

Unlike them, Thakur Udai Singhji had the good fortune of witnessing and blessing the wedlock between Jodhpur and Jaipur.

Brotherly Discord

Maharaja Abhay Singhji had just returned to Marwar with his new Kachhwaha bride to find fresh discord at home. He found that when his dejected procession returned, embers of its exclusion were rapidly fanned by the Maharaja's younger brothers, Rao Singh and Anand Singh, the chieftains who plied their disgruntled populace with splinters of a revolution against the king. Their rising flames of disdain were soon quelled by the Maharaja's loyalists led by his other brother, Rajadhiraj Bakhat Singhji of Nagaur. Thakur Udai Singhji remained undeterred in his allegiance towards the Maharaja's sovereignty and paid immediate heed to Nagaur's plea. The rebellious princes had hastily grabbed Idar and were attempting another revolt in Jalore. The situation escalated when they joined hands with the Marathas, who, under Peshwa Baji Rao I, had envisioned a northward expansion into Rajputana. Thakur Udai Singhji and his contemporaries tried their best to quell the upsurge, which was beginning to get out of hand.

In no time, the situation had cascaded out of control. Maharaja Abhay Singhji ordered Thakur Udai Singhji and Veer Durgadasji's son, Abhay Karanji, to negotiate with the Marathas. He hoped for the latter to capitalize on his father's goodwill with Khanderao, a Maratha dignitary of prominence. The duo returned with the message that the Marathas were willing to accept a peace offering worth one lakh rupees from the Maharaja, but this bid was rejected.

Instead, a three-day-long war ensued, showing not the slightest sign of submission. Marwar was eventually coerced into paying for its obstinacy with a much larger amount. Had the Maharaja agreed to pay the earlier sum demanded by the Marathas, it would have saved Marwar a devastating battle and another 1.5 lakh rupees. Evidently, Maharaja Abhay Singhji paid dearly for not heeding the advice of his two prudent men.

Several historians dismiss this incident as hearsay for its alleged miscalculations, stating that this incident sidelines the exponential strength wielded by Marwar. If at all, they consider a similar situation to have taken place at a much smaller scale, a petty rebellion at best. Moreover, they don't deny the occurrence of peaceful negotiations between the two sides but insist on Marwar upholding a more assertive stance against the Marathas.

To cite one example, Reu challenges the conviction that Thakur Udai Singhji prevailed over some Katho Peelu during the Jalore rebellion by throwing light on the fact that they were two different people. In fact, Katho Peelu was a euphemism for Kantji Kadam and Peelji Gaekwad of Baroda. Peelji Gaekwad's rebellion led to his assassination shortly after the Battle of Ahmedabad in 1732.

The Battle of Ahmedabad

Beginning as a menace for Rajputana, the Maratha advance soon grew to wreak substantial havoc for the

Rajputs. News of their disruptive advances made its way to the Mughal court. When he failed to thwart Sarbuland Khan, his recalcitrant subedar in Gujarat, Mughal emperor Nadir Shah entrusted Maharaja Abhay Singhji with his execution.

The year was 1730, and bearing a handsome sum of 18 lakh rupees from the Mughal treasury, the Maharaja led 50 cannons and an army of over 20,000 men to oust Khan. True to his name, the fearless Maharaja Abhay Singhji vowed to join his men in every military endeavour that fate thrust upon them. He marched along in his heavy battledress towards Jalore, where he was joined by his brother, Rajadhiraj Bakhat Singhji. When the brethren and their colossal armies stomped forth to behead Khan, the grounds quaked in trepidation.

When his army was just 64 miles short of Gujarat near the northern area of Sidhpur, the Maharaja swept a handful of the subedar's ex-loyalists in his favour. On a sultry October night, the Rathores arrived on the banks of the Sabarmati River and set up camp two miles away from the subedar's camp in a village called Mojir. A fully-charged Sarbuland Khan aimed his canons in their direction and triggered a surprise attack on the Rajputs. Khan's misfortune was such that his newly-turned adversaries had warned the Maharaja's army in the nick of time, and Khan's cannonballs landed on deserted soils. Maharaja Abhay Singhji had retreated by a few miles towards Khanpur well before the subedar could ignite his splinters. He dispatched his finest cavalrymen to wade across Sabarmati's waters to acquire strategic high ground around Behrampur, from where they commanded a bird's eye view of Khan's whereabouts.

Their well-targeted bombardment of Ahmedabad effectively caused Khan to scuttle with his men.

A fleeting series of high flags crowded Sarbuland Khan's field of vision. The Rajput battalion pushed him into a corner. They coerced Khan to accept defeat and enter into a treatise that made him surrender his dominion back to the Mughals.

One might ponder over Kheenvsar's direct relevance to this conquest. Kheenvsar's state archives mention this military faceoff between Maharaja Abhay Singhji and Sarbuland Khan, wherein Thakur Udai Singhji took upon the feared gladiator, Ika. When Ika's impatient sword made a clumsy stroke over his left arm, the valiant Thakur roared back, 'You know not how the sword works. Let me show you…' and cut Ika into two pieces in one stroke. When news of this incident reached him, the subedar's nephew arrogantly retorted, 'Ika's corpse doesn't vacate our fort. We will fight back!' They did so not at the active war front but by clandestinely sending an army of 5,000 to spring upon the Maharaja in his camp. Not too far away, Thakur Udai Singhji was tending to his wounds when he ascertained the impending threat. He immediately mounted his stallion and darted to Maharaja Abhay Singhji's rescue. Ghastly fatalities wracked both armies, and in the end, a meagre 35 Rajput warriors survived. Thakur Udai Singhji wasn't one of them. He took down enemy after enemy until meeting his end in present-day Bareja, 20 kilometres south of Ahmedabad city. His younger brother, Shambhu Singhji, shot Sarbuland Khan's brazen nephew dead, but if only blood could resurrect the departed.

Even after he was no more, Thakur Udai Singhji

received the Maharaja's tribute for being one of his most exalted compatriots. Furthermore, his gallantry continues to resonate in the form of songs that describe him brandishing his sword with indestructible arms as his horse arched higher than the sky. Fervent energy tightened his armour until it rattled with rage, and he wreaked havoc upon the enemies by simply glancing in their direction. He struck one spear, and the enemy's elephant came tumbling down.

Thakur Udai Singhji left behind three widowed queens, two daughters and a son, Zorawar Singhji, who rose to fill the void left by his father. His legacy was as powerful as his name.

9

Thakur Zorawar Singhji

The Greatest Statesman

A young prince back then, Thakur Zorawar Singhji fought alongside his father in the Ahmedabad war before the latter was martyred. However, the late Thakur Udai Singhji did not fall in vain. On the day that the brave Thakur was slain, Maharaja Abhay Singhji stormed the Bhadra Fort and established Rathore suzerainty over it.[1] Kheenvsar's young scion had returned to Marwar with the triumphant king and would abide by his clan's loyalty to Jodhpur in unprecedented ways.

Wherever history lacks accounts of Thakur Zorawar Singhji's combat laurels, it compensates by showering abundant praise regarding his statesmanship. The ninth thakur of Kheenvsar was known to be a formidable warrior. It is said that when he brandished his sword on the battlefield, thunder clapped in the skies above. One of his negotiatory bids forever altered Marwar's geography in its favour.

Such forthrightness is destined for worldly adulation by friends and foes alike. At the same time, virtue must often be sown in adverse soils for power to grow. Thakur Zorawar Singhji's moral uprightness and political brilliance garnered sufficient acrimony from many of his contemporaries and pushed them to perform misdemeanours that cost him his cordiality with the Jodhpur durbar. Despite earning the Maharaja's disfavour, Thakur Zorawar Singhji refused to cower. He remained resolute in his commitment to Marwar and its people.

Amidst the diplomatic oscillations Thakur Zorawar Singhji experienced in his dealings with the Jodhpur durbar, Kheenvsar was granted to the nascent capabilities of his son, Thakur Karan Singh. Fate called for Thakur Zorawar Singhji to spend most of his life either as an expatriate in Bikaner or within Marwar's multitudinous matrices of strategic arbitration. In his absence, Kheenvsar's treasury suffered erratic bouts of favour and disfavour corresponding to the Maharaja's capricious patronage.

The Hurda Gathering

Many argue that the Hurda gathering of 17 July 1734 was one of the most notable events in Rajput history. Also known as the Hurda Conference, it was a large assembly of Rajputs hosted by Sawai Jai Singhji and chaired by Mewar's Maharana Jagat Singhji II in the Hurda town of Bhilwara district. This meeting was called for the Rajputs to find an effective means of quelling the increasing Maratha advances into Rajputana. They were beginning to realize that Mughal checks and balances were failing to contain these incursions from the Deccan. If they didn't act fast enough, Rajputana faced the threat of succumbing to the Maratha dominion.

The Maharajas of Marwar, Mewar, Jaipur, Bikaner, Kota and Kishangarh and numerous other dignitaries agreed to bury their ancestral hatchets and see eye to eye for the sake of Rajput fortification. They decided to form a unified Rajput army commanded by the Maharaja of Karauli. Thakur Zorawar Singhji was part of Marwar's contingent at this momentous summit. However, before much optimism could be garnered for the future, the assembly's directives were quelled by the very internal differences they sought to override.

Rajput disunity, the factor that continues to be lamented as Rajputana's Achillean heal, abruptly ended the Hurda gathering's collective potential.

Despite Rajputana's collective failure to protect itself, Thakur Zorawar Singhji wasn't one to be demoralized. A mighty force to be reckoned with, his prudence grew increasingly sagacious and his razor-sharp wit transcended to an entirely new level.

Rathore Brothers in Arms

When Jodhpur's Maharaja Abhay Singhji began eyeing Bikaner, he was reprimanded by Nagaur's Bakhat Singhji. To salvage Rathore unity, the latter entered into an alliance with the Sawai of Jaipur. Together, they launched an offensive against Maharaja Abhay Singhji. In 1741, the armies of Jaipur and Nagaur were mobilized in Gangwana. Thakur Zorawar Singhji and a handful of Marwar's loyalists intervened in the nick of time, and the conflict was dampened by a truce by means of which Marwar averted its gaze from Bikaner.

Eight years later, the departed Maharaja's sole surviving son, Ram Singhji, faced a challenge for succession. His already unpopular reputation, coupled with his curt demeanour, swayed public support in Bakhat Singhji's favour. Amidst this feud, Thakur Zorawar Singhji lent his support to Marwar's successor by the right of primogeniture.

Even though the Karamsot carried no fondness for the unfavourable prince, his allegiance to Marwar's sovereignty superseded all matters of personal preference. News of Ram Singhji's misdeeds continued spreading rapidly, creating an ever-widening distance between him and his men. Thakur Zorawar Singhji refused to partake in this herding of loyalties.

Kheenvsar's Thakur found an aide in Indore's Malhar Rao Holkar, who graced the freshly coronated Maharaja by sending an elephant, four horses and an armour suit with 200 cavalrymen on his behalf.

The majestic sight of the Maratha elephant aroused Maharaja Ram Singhji's penchant for the sport of elephant fighting. He proposed a duel between the new entrant and one of his own elephants. So enraged was he to witness his elephant lose that he impulsively sentenced Holkar's elephant to death. The elephant was to be placed in front of the mouth of a cannon and blown into pieces. The Maharaja's inhumanity horrified Holkar's men and antagonized them to the point of rebellion.

The brutality Maharaja Ram Singhji displayed towards Holkar's generosity stunned his men beyond comprehension, and it was the Maharaja's good fortune that Riyan's Thakur Sher Singhji intermediated. The latter cajoled him out of his nefarious thoughts and insisted upon the elephant's symbolism as Lord Ganesha. *How could a king of virtue indulge in the ominous slaughter of an animal this sacred, especially when it has been presented to him? If His Highness felt repulsed by the magnificent beast, why not hand it down to one of his treasured men?*

On hearing the judicious Thakur's words, the Maharaja desisted from his diabolical whim and handed over the elephant to his blue-eyed clansman, Thakur Zorawar Singhji. He also made a requital of elephants to each of his aristocrats of Pokhran, Auwa, Aasop, Pali, Kosana, Nimaj, Riyan and 11 other fiefdoms.

The Battle of Raona (Pipar)

On 23 June 1724, Maharaja Ajit Singhji was murdered in cold blood by his son, Bakhat Singhji, while he lay asleep.[2] It is argued that this assassination was planned by both his sons to erase their rebelling father and appease the Mughal court that viewed Ajit Singhji with contempt for his disobedient ways. The two brothers hoped to win succession over Jodhpur, even if it meant sacrificing their father.

The deceased Maharaja Ajit Singhji's firstborn, Abhay Singhji, had been representing him at the Mughal court in Delhi and was proclaimed king shortly after the incident in July. By the power vested in him by the Mughal emperor, he was now the ruler of Marwar, including Nagaur.

In the following month, the newly crowned Maharaja proceeded to Mathura to wed Jaipur's Sawai Jai Singhji's daughter. By virtue of this wedlock, Maharaja Abhay Singhji hoped to garner the patronage of the most influential Rajput ruler at the time.

However, Marwar lacked a strong king, and civil unrest began to brew. Maharaja Abhay Singhji was losing allies. His brothers, Anand and Raj Singhji, rebelled against him and declared themselves independent, while another brother claimed Jalore. Marwar's security and sanctity lay scattered amidst these feuds, and Maharaja Abhay Singhji cried out to the Mughal emperor for help, who, in turn, relied on Sawai Jai Singhji to restore peace in Marwar.

Maharaja Abhay Singhji eventually managed to quell the rebellion to some extent with the help of Jaipur. It was an uphill task because his rebelling brothers were backed by Maratha chieftains, such as Kanthaji Kadam and Pilaji Gaekwad. Together, they pillaged several parts of Jalore. These two brothers were eventually placated in 1728 when they were granted supremacy over Idar.

Amidst recovering much of what had been lost, Maharaja Abhay Singhji granted the lordship of Nagaur to his brother, Bakhat Singhji, in 1729 CE. Jaipur's assistance upon Mughal behest had been instrumental in Marwar's stability at this juncture. In repayment of their support, the Mughals deployed Maharaja Abhay Singhji as the governor of Gujarat from 1730 to 1737 CE.

Marwar's Feud with Bikaner

Shortly after assuming lordship over Nagaur, Bakhat Singhji began demanding concessions from Bikaner. The then Raja of Bikaner sent word to Sawai Jai Singh II in Jaipur, hoping to earn his patronage. Jaipur's advice that Raja Abhay Singhji ease Marwar's stance towards Bikaner was in vain. The prudent Sawai negotiated with Bakhat Singhji instead and succeeded in cajoling him by granting him a monetary peace offering and the town of Merta. With Bakhat Singhji out of the way, Jaipur was in a commanding position to force Maharaja Abhay Singhji into peace. Now devoid of his younger brother's support against Jaipur, Maharaja Abhay Singhji was forced to comply. Marwar suffered heavy reparations to Jaipur and the Mughals, and its diminished power was further highlighted with Jaipur eclipsing its stature in the Mughal court. Several Rathores grew enraged by Marwar's compromised position and blamed Bakhat Singhji for these circumstances.

Marwar made a retributive effort in the Batte of Gangwana (1741 CE) when the two brothers reunited against Jaipur. Bakhat Singhji expressed remorse for his earlier abandonment and contributed a large cavalry to fight the Sawai's forces. Both sides suffered heavy casualties, and Marwar emerged as the victor. Sawai Jai Singhji was forced to accept Maharaja Abhay Singhji's peace terms and return home utterly dejected.

Bakhat Singhji's battle time valour and meteoric rise earned him fame and recognition from the people of Marwar. Initially, Bakhat Singhji had served his brother as a staunch supporter and loyal ally. However, upon returning from his deputation to Gujarat, it is said that the Maharaja took to drinking heavily and his equation with his erstwhile loyal brother began to change. Demeaning Maharaja Abhay Singhji as an unworthy ruler, Bakhat Singhji began to harbour ambitions of ascending the throne himself. Thus, when Abhay Singhji breathed his last in 1749, Bakhat Singhji marched towards Jodhpur and ousted the deceased king's son, Ram Singhji, in his claim for supreme power.

Ram Singhji reacted by soliciting Maratha support. They and Thakur Zorawar Singhji arrived to negotiate, but when their alliance failed to retrieve Jodhpur from Bakhat Singhji, Ram Singhji sought asylum in Jaipur and Thakur Zorawar Singhji departed for Bikaner.

In 1750, the Mir Bakshi, Salabat Khan, unleashed a fresh offensive in a pursuit to capture Marwar.[3] Ram Singhji turned to Jaipur and received Sawai Ishwari Singhji's support in the war. Ram Singhji's army, combined with the forces mobilized for him in Jaipur, totalled 30,000 men and abundant artillery. They advanced towards Pipar, towards the south of Merta. Salabat Khan's army camped at Raona, about seven miles to their east.

After eight days of little warfare but extensive negotiations, Salabat Khan finally decided to attack Ram Singhji's men. That, too, ceased after four hours, with the Sawai brokering a peace accord. Salabat Khan retreated after the Sawai promised him a handsome sum of 27 lakhs, and Marwar was relieved of Mughal offensives for the time being.

Merta War

Royal intrigue engulfed Marwar once again when Bakhat Singhji's son, Vijay Singhji, wrongly occupied Maharaja Ram Singhji's throne. Resentful of Vijay Singhji, Maharaja Ram Singhji retaliated in 1754 CE by forging an alliance involving Thakur Zorawar Singhji, Dalji Kumpawat and the Maratha ruler Jayappaji Scindia of Gwalior.[4]

Scindia directed an army of 60,000 men against Vijay Singhji to uphold the Jodhpur durbar's cause. Vijay Singhji, who was now accompanied by the kings of Bikaner and Kishangarh, counterattacked with a force of 40,000 in Gangrana, a village southwest of Merta. When push came to shove, Vijay Singhji killed Jayappaji Scindia by treachery, but his son, Jankoji Scindia, prevailed with Thakur Zorawar Singhji and Dalji Kumpawat in protecting Jodhpur.

By now, Vijay Singhji had been coerced into an armistice with Maharaja Ram Singhji, which ordered Vijay Singhji to pay a reparative sum of 50 lakh rupees to the Scindias and give the valuable province of Ajmer.

The rest of Marwar was to be divided into two halves. Jodhpur and Nagaur were granted to Vijay Singhji, whereas Merta, Jalore, Maroth, Sojat, Sambar, Parbatsar and several other districts were to be retained by Maharaja Ram Singhji. Maharaja Ram Singhji made his way to Jaipur in 1756, where nuptial celebrations awaited him. Many years ago, when he was still a child, Sawai Isri Singhji of Jaipur had pledged him his daughter's hand. Now that the princess had blossomed into a woman, it was time for the couple to exchange garlands. Needless to mention, Thakur Zorawar Singhji wouldn't let his king go unescorted.

Filial Oscillations

The newlyweds were settling into their fort in Merta under the queen mother's guardianship when a note arrived from Jodhpur. It was a confidential note for Thakur Zorawar Singhji and several vassals in a deliberate attempt to weaken their allegiance towards Maharaja Ram Singhji. Maharaja Vijay Singhji's scheme got the better of Thakur Zorawar Singhji, but instead of obliging him in Jodhpur, he sought refuge in Bikaner. His unyielding temperament and candid predisposition stung feudal egos and brewed jealousy that echoed till the Jodhpur durbar. For the next four years, Thakur Zorawar Singhji's distant posting seemed to placate his envious comrades. However, neither Jodhpur's Maharaja nor his charlatans felt his prolonged absence because Kheenvsar's Thakur was making a comeback.

The Champawat Rebellion

An alternate account narrates that in 1760, Maharaja Vijay Singhji invited his aristocrats on the occasion of his guru's passing. The distinguished sage Atmaramji's ashes were to be hallowed, for which the thakurs of Raas, Pokhran, Aasop and Nimaj made a timely arrival. It was only after they had stepped through the innermost gate of Mehrangarh that they realized this ceremony was a trap. Within six days, Devi Singhji, the Thakur Sahib of Pokaran, passed away. The Thakur Sahib of Aasop departed for the heavens in the same month. Maharaja Vijay Singhji released the Thakur of Nimaj on juvenile grounds. These unjust detentions and deaths caused a massive uproar across Marwar.

Devi Singhji's son, Sambal Singhji, and his fellow Champawats were embittered and furious enough at Maharaja Vijay Singhji to seek bloody revenge. The hostile Champawats' advance from Pokhran rang alarm bells in the durbar. Maharaja Vijay Singhji frantically appealed to Thakur Zorawar Singhji to intervene.

In due course, Kheenvsar's treasury swelled with copious incentives from Marwar to secure, offered its thakur's favour. The fact that Kheenvsar's finances doubled in a single year spoke volumes of its thakur's indispensability to Marwar. The Karamsot bid to restore peace amongst his Champawat brothers prevailed, and Jodhpur heaved a sigh of relief.

With the advent of his meteoric popularity, Thakur Zorawar Singhji formed close ties with the then Prime Minister Surat Mal. Together, they made meaningful ripples in the many spheres of Marwar's administration.

This newborn alliance attracted the scorn of titular officers, who began poisoning Maharaja Vijay Singhji's mind once again. Their deliberate slander threatened the Maharaja's insecurities, and there came a point when he could no longer mask this freshly brewed antagonism.

Thakur Zorawar Singhji was perceptive enough to recognize the alterations in Maharaja Vijay Singhji's demeanour, and after a verbal spat with one of the royal attachés in Bhakri in 1764, he once again departed for Bikaner. Perhaps his duties to Jodhpur had been duly fulfilled, and his usefulness to the Maharaja had ended. Thus commenced his four-year-long sojourns in Bikaner. It was only after he had departed that the Maharaja felt a deep sense of remorse for failing to trust his cherished Karamsot leader. In a placatory effort, Maharaja Vijay Singhji exempted Thakur Zorawar Singhji's son from the stately taxes levied on horse and camel trading. Nevertheless, the proud Thakur dismissed this apparent act of magnanimity and chose to persist in solitude.

To Mewar's Rescue in Lieu of Godwar

Mewar had lost its Maharana, Raj Singhji II, without a successor. His uncle, Ari Singhji II, assumed supreme power over the kingdom, but *Eklingji's* divine providence shepherded the late Maharana's infant, whom his widow birthed. The late Maharana's rightful heir, Ratan Singh, had entered the world, throwing open the debate on Mewar's rightful heir.

Ratan Singh was backed by several nobles, and thanks to a newly acquired alliance with the Marathas, the late Maharana's cause was upheld. Mewar was divided into two halves, with one half being granted to Ari Singhji II and the other half, which included Kumbhalgarh, went to Ratan Singhji.

Doleful and roused by a sense of depravity, Ari Singhji II sought Jodhpur's support in lieu of Godwar, a highly strategic region of geopolitical advantage. He entrusted the Maharaja with a joint cavalry and infantry force of 3,000, which was stationed 50 kilometres southwest of Kumbhalgarh in the Vaishnav pilgrimage site of Nathdwara. Alas, even with the combined efforts of Jodhpur, Ari Singhji II failed to retrieve Kumbhalgarh. In the face of this initial impasse, Maharaja Vijay Singhji amassed some of his finest men to pursue Ari Singhji II's cause. With enduring help from Bikaner's Maharaja, he welcomed Thakur Zorawar Singhji into his camp yet again. To assuage the latter, he went out of his way to throw a grand welcome at Siwana, where Thakur Zorawar Singhji arrived while returning to Jodhpur.

Thereafter, in 1770, the Maharajas of Jodhpur, Bikaner and Kishangarh arrived at Nathdwara in the hope of reinvigorating their stagnant armies but to no avail. One day, as the Maharajas were offering their prayers at Shrinathji's shrine, a frustrated Ari Singhji II blustered, 'You've taken away Godwar from me but haven't been able to live up to your commitment in return! Therefore, it would be fitting for you to return Godwar to Mewar!' Caught off-guard, Maharaja Vijay Singhji stood dumbfounded until Thakur Zorawar Singhji snapped back, 'Godwar now remains tied to the heads of over 50,000 Rathores. Come retain it if you have the courage to sever each one of these heads. When the last Rathore head falls limply against the ground, consider Godwar yours again.' To date, this incident reflects Thakur Zorawar Singhji's mettle and candour. After all, for a Thakur to sternly tell off Mewar's aspiring ruler was not an act for the faint-hearted.

The Kheenvsar Haveli

Godwar was thus retained and safeguarded within Marwar's map thanks to its boldest son. Maharaja Vijay Singhji remained indebted towards Kheenvsar's Thakur for his act and expressed his gratitude by granting him a *haveli* near Toorji ka Jhalra. This dwelling came to be known as Kheenvsar Haveli.

Another anecdote surfaces at this juncture, which is retold to commemorate the Thakur's largesse. When the Kheenvsar Haveli was commissioned, it was to be secured with a boundary wall, which, for some reason, remained undone. Its absence left the haveli's borders ambiguous, and over the following months, a sizeable cluster of Jat settlements mushroomed there. In 1771, Maharaja Vijay Singhji recalled this unfinished task and ordered its completion.

Where would the Jat settlers go?

What weight could a handful of plebians levy against the royal order?

Before they could be overruled, Kheenvsar's Thakur made an earnest plea to the Maharaja to revoke his judgement so that the Jats were not displaced. They were on the verge of destitution, and if a wall was erected, they would be rendered homeless. Instead of forcefully eradicating them, Thakur Zorawar Singhji proposed a gentler approach with which the Jats could be made aware of the situation and incentivized to resettle. Compensatory land and money would be offered to them by the durbar so that their interests weren't jeopardized.

One must note that Thakur Zorawar Singhji was at the zenith of his popularity at this point. He could have easily basked in the Maharaja's favourability and accepted a fortification of his haveli. On the contrary, he lacked the slightest sense of entitlement and ensured a dignified and just solution to the matter.

Second Only to One

It was only in 1772 that the Jodhpur durbar granted the Thakur permission to return to Kheenvsar. To Maharaja Vijay Singhji's surprise, the Karamsot Thakur politely declined his offer and chose to remain in Jodhpur. The former received this announcement with sheer exuberance and joy. To express his mirth, he adorned Thakur Zorawar Singhji with bountiful gifts and a golden sword embedded with precious gems.

An eminent quote that can be modified to shower praise on Thakur Zorawar Singhji goes, 'You can take the Karamsot out of Kheenvsar, but you cannot take Kheenvsar out of the Karamsot.' The ninth Karamsot scion had upheld his familial allegiance, and so unyielding was his virtue that Marwar's historians place him second only to the legendary Veer Durgadasji. His priceless acquisition of Godwar and other parts of Mewar as indefinite annexations in Marwar's favour receive praise till date. Maharaja Gaj Singhji II of Marwar has appreciated this particular contribution of the Karamsots on numerous occasions.

THE PALACE,
JODHPUR.

॥श्री जलधरनाथजी सहाय है॥

स्वस्ति श्री सकल सुभ ओपमा लायक राजराजेश्वर महाराजाधिराज महाराजा श्री श्री १००८ श्री गजसिंघजी सा. चि. युवराज श्री श्री १०५ श्री शिवराजसिंघजी सा. मारवाड़. जोधपुर देव वचनायत पाथ तखतगढ़. जोधपुर खींवसर रा पटायत सदामद मारवाड़ रा सामधरमी आठ मिसला रा ठिकाणा में भेला रहेया ने घणी बंदगीया करने जस रा भागीदार रहेया।

राव जोधाजी रा नवमा बेटा राव करमसी रै लारे करमसोत राठौड़ केविंजिया ने इणा रो पाट घर खिंवसर ठिकाणो रहेयो।

जोधपुर री गादी मांयै टीकायत थरपणा में मिसला रै पटायतो रो सरावण जोग हाथ रहेयो। मारवाड़ रा महाराजा बिजैसिंघजी रै राज में गोढवाड़ री रुखाली राखता थका खिंवसर रा जद रा पटायत ठाकर जोरावरसिंघ जी पठाणा ने बधारता थका कयो के "थारा राणाजी नूं कहे के गोढवाड़ बाता साठे आई ही सो पाछी माथा साठे आवसी।"

खिंवसर रा पटायत ठाकर ओंकारसिंघजी करमसोत राठौड़ ने वा रै पूरवजा री बंदगीया री सरावण जोग ने आज रा जमाना में नाम कमावण रै मांयै राजदरबार मारवाड़ सूं सामधरम ने हेत इखलास सूं भेला रहेया, जिण सूं राजी होय ने जूनी परमपरा री पदवी 'राजा' रो खिताब दरबार मारवाड़. जोधपुर तारीख २९ अक्टूबर २००७, संवत् २०६४, वार सोमवार तिथि चतुर्थी कातिक मास से दिन राजी होय ने हुक्म बख्शायो।

गजसिंह
महाराजा, मारवाड-जोधपुर

His Highness Maharaja Gaj Singhji's letter that restored Kheenvsar to its rank as a sirayat and conferred upon Onkar Singhji the title of Raja. The letter also mentions Thakur Zorawar Singhji's role in Marwar's recovery of Godwar.

Second to none in his patriotism towards Jodhpur, Thakur Zorawar Singhji was not only a statesman of great eminence but also a charitable noble of his times. He empathized with the downtrodden and made several efforts for their upliftment.

A keen admirer of poetry, he was also particularly interested in several architectural genres.

Informal state records point towards Kheenvsar Fort's completion in his era. He not only propelled the fortification of Karamsots through strategic dialogue but also maintained strong ties with Bikaner and the formidable Marathas.

There are specific mentions of Thakur Zorawar Singhji's prudent defence of Nagaur's Bhadora village against the advances of Peshwa Madhavrao I.

One anecdote that illustrates his deep sense of philanthropy unfolded when Kheenvsar received an unannounced visitor. Sandu Jalam Singhji arrived at the Thakur's doorstep without any prior notification. Zorawar Singhji was in the middle of his daily puja rituals, completely unaware that Jalam Singhji was waiting for him outside. When he finished his prayers and stepped out, he learned of the incident. Jalam Singhji had been unwilling to wait on him and had left in a huff. Thakur Zorawar Singhji immediately called for Jalam Singhji to return and tended to him without further delay.

Once he had resolved the issues that Jalam Singhji had approached him for, he received the latter's sincere apologies for the rude remarks he had made earlier.

The fact that Sandu Tej Singhji, another resident of Bhadora, documented this anecdote highlights Thakur Zorawar Singhji's strong ties with the village.

Even though Thakur Zorawar Singhji spent most of his life away from Kheenvsar, it was here that he returned to breathe his last. He was mourned in 1772, and two of his five queens committed sati. Their memory remains enshrined in two adjoining chhatris on the banks of Padamsar.

A stone inscription under Thakur Zorawar Singhji's chhatri, where he is mounted on a horse. Standing beside him is his queen.

10

Thakur Karan Singhji

The Unwavering Sentinel

The void caused by Thakur Zorawar Singhji's enduring absence from Kheenvsar was soothed by his son, Karan Singhji, from a tender age. As per Marwar's age-old protocols, a deceased ruler's successor can assume royal office only after it has been conferred upon him by the Maharaja in person. Until then, the scion remains a provisional figure in waiting.

Jodhpur's Maharaja Vijay Singhji arrived in Kheenvsar on a cold February day in 1772 to perform his stately duties. He affectionately accepted the *amal ka dastoor* from Karan Singhji's cupped hands. Maharaja Vijay Singhji pinned a colourfully studded *sirpech* onto Karan Singhji's safa and, with the generous bequeathal of 31 villages to Kheenvsar, proclaimed him the 10th torchbearer of the Karamsot dynasty. Thakur Karan Singhji's first cordial encounter with the Maharaja would also be his last.

A Black Day for Marwar

The bygone animosities between Jodhpur and Kheenvsar resurfaced within five years after Thakur Karan Singhji's coronation. History was repeating itself in an uncanny manner. Like his father, Thakur Karan Singhji drifted away from the Maharaja's tutelage due to diplomatic convulsions. Chronicles point to one instance that likely sparked the impending stalemates.

By 1773, news of the unlawful acts committed by Auwa's Jait Singh Champawat had travelled far and wide. As a corrective measure, Maharaja Vijay Singhji summoned several Rathore chieftains to his durbar. Amongst them were the thakurs of Khairwa, Pokhran and Kheenvsar and the infamous Thakur from Auwa. Jodhpur's royal henchman, Singhvi Khoobchand, kept a hawkish eye on the thakurs as they prostrated before the Maharaja. When Jait Singhji was paying his respects to the king, Khoobchand struck him twice on his back and the alleged outlaw fell dead in a pool of blood.

Maharaja Vijay Singhji's villainous means of executing the miscreant Thakur astonished and terrorized the remaining thakurs. They shuddered upon recalling that the royal court had recently prohibited such killings as unlawful acts. Amidst the anarchy, Khairwa's Thakur warned his co-spectators, 'All those who disobey his Majesty shall suffer the same outcome!' However, the hypocrisy didn't end there. Five hundred cavalrymen from the royal barracks rode alongside Singhvi Vanechand, another one of the Maharaja's bounty hunters, to capture Auwa. Thakur Karan Singhji responded in the only manner befitting this treachery: with shock, disapproval and disgust.

This fateful day is marked in black in Marwar's annals. Unsurprisingly, impressions of a just durbar ceased to exist in the collective conscience of Marwar's many thikanas. Even though it was the duty of every Karamsot to pledge allegiance to Jodhpur, Thakur Karan Singhji felt it against his principles to serve a deceitful man, irrespective of his exalted and royal stature. Thus, when conflicting loyalties towards Jodhpur gave rise to two factions, he joined the opposition. Maharaja Vijay Singhji was disappointed to witness Kheenvsar's hostile position. His sycophants merely fanned the embers of his suspicions until a fire began to rage.

Jodhpur Attacks Kheenvsar

Tides of rebellion against the durbar were gaining wind in Raipur and Kheenvsar.[1] Maharaja Vijay Singhji sought to quell this, and after a 15-day-long offensive at Raipur, he ordered his contingent to proceed towards Kheenvsar to destroy it.

Kheenvsar's growing influence in the area was beginning to vex Maharaja Vijay Singhji, so he dispatched a representative, Singhvi Khoobchand, to Thakur Karan Singhji. 'Punctuating the barren expanse between Jodhpur and Nagaur, your edifice at Kheenvsar stings the Maharaja's eyes,' he said. Khoobchand's contemporary, Singhvi Bheemraj, obeyed the royal command and laid siege to Kheenvsar Fort. Well aware that Marwar had sent advanced weaponry to bring them down, the Karamsot defence stood fearless. Thakur Karan Singhji sent for his younger brother, Bhom Singhji, who, at the time, was on a military deputation at the Marwar–Jaisalmer border. Despite their primitive weapons, the brave army of Karamsots stood their ground for six long months. To strike a decisive blow on the unrelenting Karamsots, Jodhpur supplemented its camp with state-of-the-art cannons granted to them by the Mughals. These cannons bore advanced technology capable of catapulting heavy rocks and cannonballs, a weapon for which Kheenvsar had no defence.

The resilient fort of the Karamsots, which had weathered the devastating months of warfare, finally began to crumble in 1779. Thakur Karan Singhji and his trusted brethren lost all remaining hope and were compelled to flee for their lives. They sought refuge in Bikaner under his father's ally, Maharaja Rai Singhji.

No sooner had the Karamsots' wounds begun to heal in Bikaner than their homeland was annexed by the Maharaja and granted to Singhvi Bheemraj at the Maharaja's durbar.

Our Eternal Vanguard: Bikaner

Bikaner's sovereign, Maharaja Rai Singhji, welcomed his vanquished cousins with open arms. True to his ancestral charity towards Kheenvsar, he hosted Thakur Karan Singhji and his troops with utmost care. He even upheld his father's promise of passing on the two villages meant for late Thakur Zorawar Singhji. They were duly granted to Thakur Karan Singhji and Bhom Singhji, for whom these lands served as crucial assets of sustenance. The revenue they earned from these fodder grounds financed them through their long refuge.

The Battle of Merta

Thakur Karan Singhji spent his last days with dignity identical to his father's.

On 10 September 1790, Jodhpur was bracing itself against another Maratha assault backed by French General Benoît De Boigne.

The Scindias and Holkars had jointly vanquished the Tomars of Patan, after which they demanded that Marwar hand them the reins of Ajmer. Maharaja Vijay Singhji's reluctance to part with this strategic city incited the Scindias to direct an offensive against Marwar. Maharaja Vijay Singhji conscripted his Rajput subjects to contend with the Maratha advance, which faced temporary entrapment while crossing the Luni River. In their reluctance to be the first to attack, the Marwar troops accorded their enemy camp sufficient time to retrieve their artillery from the Luni and advance swiftly towards Merta. Before the crack of dawn, De Boigne's men launched a surprise attack on the Jodhpur infantry. Bhimraj Bakshi, the commander of the Jodhpur army, saw no prospects against De Boigne's mighty forces and fled from the scene.

With primitive weapons and a leaderless order, the Rajputs put up a short-lived but brave fight before De Boigne occupied Merta Fort. The aggressors plundered the fort and brought the Maharaja's men to their knees. The Maharajas of Bikaner and Kishangarh were cognizant of the unabating force at hand. It was impossible for Marwar to supersede De Boigne by force, and a truce was the only way out. Heeding their prudent advice, Maharaja Vijay Singhji pleaded with the Marathas for a peace treaty, but the latter refused to negotiate with him. The two sides were stuck in an impasse. The Marathas were ready to discuss a settlement only with the kindred of the late Thakur Zorawar Singhji.

In his time, Thakur Zorawar Singhji was among the rare Rathore chieftains to have gained Maratha adulation. He had even exchanged turbans with the Marathas in an officiation of brotherly ties with them. However, Jodhpur's Maharaja was too late in sending for Thakur Zorawar Singhji's son. To its unsurmountable loss, Jodhpur's royal messenger returned empty-handed from Bikaner because Thakur Zorawar Singhji's son and grandson were no more.

11

Thakur Berisal Singhji

A Thakur Gone Too Soon

Kheenvsar's 11th scion, Thakur Berisal Singhji, was possibly the youngest Karamsot supremo when he departed for the heavens. He breathed his last only a year after losing his father. For the little time that Thakur

Berisal Singhji lived, he, too, sought asylum in Bikaner like his father and grandfather. Maharaja Rai Singhji honourably upheld his custodianship by passing on the late Thakur's inheritances to his 21-year-old son, who was lost to an untimely death in 1789. Thakur Berisal Singhji lived to the age of 22 years.

Kheenvsar under Its Chhutbhai Karamsots

Thakur Bhom Singhji Zorawarsinghot[1]

With the consecutive loss of its two scions, Kheenvsar's future lay in the juvenile hands of five-year-old Bhopal Singhji. Thakur Zorawar Singhji's second son and Thakur Berisal Singhji's younger brother, Thakur Bhom Singhji, assumed charge of his homeland until his nephew came of age to serve Kheenvsar with the prudence befitting its thakur.

Upon being overpowered by the Maharaja's army in Kheenvsar, Bhom Singhji rushed to seek shelter in Bikaner along with his kinsfolk. Soon after besieging Kheenvsar, Jodhpur took hold of his jagir, Panchodi, as well.

Karma would play its role in due time. In the impasse at Merta, Mahadji Shinde summoned the sons of his cherished friend, the late Thakur Zorawar Singhji, to the negotiation table. The frantic Maharaja's messenger reached Bikaner only to find Thakur Bhom Singhji as the sole remnant of Kheenvsar's legacy for the time being. Even though Maharaja Vijay Singhji had been the chief perpetrator of his family's exile, Thakur Bhom Singhji upheld the magnanimous Karamsot legacy and departed to oblige the royal command. In Merta, he succeeded in ending the impasse between Marwar on one side and the Marathas with General De Boigne on the other. Maharaja Vijay Singhji eventually conceded Ajmer to the Marathas along with a mammoth penalty of 60 lakh rupees. In return, Mahadji Shinde ordered his army to retreat. Marwar was once again rescued by its unconditionally loyal sentinels from Kheenvsar.

This gesture by the transient Karamsot leader triggered a relaxation of ties between Kheenvsar and Jodhpur. Maharaja Vijay Singhji expressed remorse for his previous misjudgement and returned Kheenvsar and Panchodi to their rightful heirs. Whether Thakur Bhom Singhji reacquired Kheenvsar through peaceful negotiations with the Marathas and whether he was holding fort for his young nephew is unclear. More concrete accounts of history state that Kheenvsar's devout codes of primogeniture were deliberately flouted by two generations after Thakur Berisal Singhji's death. Late Thakur Zorawar Singhji's second son, Thakur Bhom Singhji, assumed governorship over Kheenvsar, and instead of granting it to Bhopal Singhji, he chose his son, Thakur Pratap Singhji, as his successor.

The father–son duo succeeded in winning back many of their family's villages they had lost to Marwar. In fact, Thakur Bhom Singhji's political clout grew exponentially, and numerous statesmen became affiliated with him in their pursuit of Maharaja Vijay Singhji's favour. One such dignitary even donated a reparation fund for the dilapidated fort walls.

A climate of realpolitik descended upon Marwar's political affairs, and Thakur Bhom Singhji treaded these precarious times with utmost caution. Grateful as he was to the Maharaja for his generosity, he was shrewd enough to discern Jodhpur's ulterior motives. He was aware that Marwar had relaxed its stance towards the Karamsots because of their irreplaceable diplomatic and negotiation capabilities. Upon discovering this logic, Thakur Bhom Singhji refrained from placing more faith in the Maharaja. Instead, he patiently waited for a chance to switch sides. As luck would have it, a fresh coup against Maharaja Vijay Singhji was brewing in Jodhpur, led by Bhim Singhji, his grandson.

Pokhran's Thakur Sawai Singhji led the anti-loyalist faction and proclaimed Bhim Singhji as Marwar's *yuvraj.* Jodhpur's newly proclaimed regent, Bhim Singhji, went on to occupy Mehrangarh, which served as his dwelling for the following year. After that, he was departing for Siwana when Maharaja Vijay Singhji's army intercepted him en route, causing a skirmish in Jhanwar. Much to the Maharaja's dismay, Thakur Bhom Singhji had outrightly sided with the young prince and challenged the royal army.

Marwar lost Maharaja Vijay Singhji in the midst of this feud, and Bhim Singhji occupied his throne without any delay. Kheenvsar's Thakur was amongst the new king's chosen men and was even seen accompanying the new Maharaja on his royal howdah. Maharaja Bhim Singhji rewarded his loyalty from time to time and issued a royal ordinance to maintain Thakur Bhom Singhji's sovereignty over the villages that had faced recent challenges.

Inscriptions on a chhatri in Padamsar indicate that 1796 CE marked Thakur Bhom Singhji's final year. His death was followed by one of his queens, Jadechiji, committing sati. His son, Pratap Singhji, replaced him as the thakur of Kheenvsar.

Thakur Pratap Singhji Bhomsinghot

Kheenvsar's new custodian, Thakur Pratap Singhji, did not share his father's affiliation vis-à-vis Maharaja Bhim Singhji for reasons that are not well known. Their soured relations are displayed in the latter's confiscation of his inheritance. However, this sabotage was promptly salvaged by Marwar's new Maharaja, Man Singhji. Due to his revocation of Bhim Singhji's actions, Maharaja Man Singhji found that when Jaipur, Bikaner, Kishangarh and Pokhran opposed his ascendancy, Kheenvsar refrained from joining the lot. In this context, two letters dated between 1806 and 1807, addressed to Thakur Pratap Singhji from the Maharaja, have been recorded. By means of this communication, the Maharaja requested Kheenvsar's Thakur to let bygones be bygones and uphold his ancestral loyalty towards the house of Marwar.[2] Similar chronicles reverberate Maharaja Man Singhji's fond regard for Kheenvsar. To bury the hatchet, the former awarded several jagirs to Thakur Pratap Singhji. On one occasion, it is believed that the latter was the lucky recipient of a string of pearls given to him by the durbar.

Given this backdrop of unquestionable felicity, it is indeed surprising that animosities sprouted between the two sides within the next two years. Although historical records do not clarify the reasons, Maharaja Man Singhji seized all of Thakur Pratap Singhji's assets and handed them over to his cousin, Bhopal Singhji. By now, the late Thakur Karan Singhji's heir apparent had reached an age to reclaim his primogenitary rights as Kheenvsar's 12th ruler by direct descent. History would come to know him as Thakur Bhopal Singhji.

12

Thakur Bhopal Singhji

The Rebel King

After Thakur Berisal Singhji's demise, his five-year-old son was raised singlehandedly by his widow, Thakurani Agar Kanwar Rajawat, in Panchodi. A temple she consecrated in this village stands tall even today. Bhopal Singhji had rendered his services to Marwar well before Maharaja Man Singhji and proclaimed him as Kheenvsar's rightful inheritor. In fact, he was seen accompanying Man Singhji's predecessor, Maharaja Bhim Singhji, on important occasions, such as his wedding processions towards Lakhasar and Jaipur. Young as he had been, Bhopal Singhji joined his fellow Rathore chieftains in wearing groomsmen attires. They collectively flanked the dashing Maharaja in a picturesque formation.

Just as he had rejoiced in many of Marwar's wedding ceremonies, he also came to the Maharaja's aid during matrimonial intrigues. One prominent incident occurred upon the untimely demise of Maharaja Bhim Singhji, who left behind his fiancée, Princess Krishna Kumari of Mewar. Her father, the Maharana, then decided to pursue her wedlock with the Sawai of Jaipur, which Jodhpur vehemently opposed. In retaliation, Maharaja Man Singhji decided to set up a military camp in Naand near Merta. Here, he found a close aide in Jaswantrao Holkar, the Maharaja of Indore. The duo was joined by Sirohi's Indraraj Singhi to combat Jaipur's army, which had now begun to advance in their direction.

More pragmatic men on both sides considered it best if a military showdown was avoided altogether. Indraraj Singhi, who was a Diwan at the Jodhpur durbar and later a chief in Maharaja Man Singh's court, represented Jodhpur in a peaceful negotiation with Jaipur's Diwan Raichand. With this exchange and the resulting truce, Marwar and Jaipur ceded their aspirations for Udaipur's princess.

Maharaja Man Singhji was retreating towards Merta

when a rival faction of kinsmen blockaded him at Parbatsar. Pokhran's Sawai Singhji had formed alliances with Bikaner, Kishangarh and even Jaipur to oppose him. The leader of this faction, Dhonkal Singhji, was the late Maharaja Bhim Singhji's legitimate heir, whose kingship was sabotaged by Maharaja Man Singhji. Several chieftains, who stood in the Maharaja's favour, hastily arrived to defend him and pleaded that better wisdom was in permitting the opposition to play out. This view received the nods of Auwa, Aasop, Nimaj, Raas, Aahor, Kuchaman and Khejarla.

At the time, Kheenvsar maintained a slightly more complex stance. Even though Thakur Bhopal Singhji stood by the Maharaja until he returned to Jodhpur, he, too, joined Dhonkal Singhji's camp and refused to budge despite Maharaja Man Singhji's numerous letters. When the Maharaja's adversaries captured Jodhpur in 1807, Maharaja Man Singhji released Indraraj Singhi from prison to consolidate Marwar's defence. Singhi forged an alliance with Aamir Khan Pindari, the Nawab of Tonk, to launch an attack so formidable that even the Sawai fled from his camp.

Together, they secured Jodhpur, and Singhi flexed his bargaining power to bring Thakur Bhopal Singhji on Maharaja Man Singhji's side. This brokered peace between the two men was short-lived. Kheenvsar's equanimity with Jodhpur reached another stalemate during the Gingoli agitation of 1807. Thakur Bhopal Singhji and his uncle, Durjan Singhji, protested for Dhonkal Singhji's cause once again. In return, they lost all their territories to the Maharaja as a punitive action for their mutiny.

Archival records point to Maharaja Man Singh addressing as many as six letters to Kheenvsar around that time, imploring its Thakur to uphold his duties towards Jodhpur. Even though Jodhpur was no longer in immediate danger, Maharaja Man Singhji appealed for his clansman's help to fortify it against impending threats. He even tried to placate Thakur Bhopal Singhji with monetary incentives and eventually transferred Kheenvsar from his uncle, Thakur Pratap Singhji, back to him. This appears to be the primary reason for Thakur Pratap Singhji favouring Pokhran-led rebels. His diplomatic stance can be read as an explicit expression of spite against Marwar for this displacement of privilege.

The year after the Gingoli protests, the freshly enthroned Thakur Bhopal Singhji had begun developing a favourable outlook towards Jodhpur. A few months before attaining Kheenvsar, the Karamsot Thakur obliged the royal command of representing Marwar amidst an ongoing altercation with the Maharao of Sirohi. Before Thakur Bhopal Singhji departed for military service, Maharaja Man Singhji is believed to have honoured him with a sword and draped a scarf around his nape. Evidence of their enduring solidarity can be found in the Maharaja's timely arrival to condole Thakurani Agar Kanwar's death in 1818. In the same year, Maharaja Man Singhji suffered the tragic bereavement of his son, Yuvraj Chhatra Singhji, in a local rebellion. In addition to bearing this insurmountable loss, he was duty-bound to atone for it by continuing to render royal services to Marwar, when he might far rather have sought solitude in hermitage. Thakur Bhopal Singhji personally shared in the grieving Maharaja's sorrow but once again went astray in 1820.

After such profound episodes of solidarity, it was surprising to observe Thakur Bhopal Singhji's noble virtues turning rogue. He and his uncle, Durjan Singhji, disrupted their neighbourhood with repeated pillages. Maharaja Man Singhji took punitive action against their misdeeds and, under the charade of a private assembly, sentenced them to a five-year-long term in Mehrangarh's Salimkot Prison.[1] As mentioned earlier, Kheenvsar and Panchodi were confiscated as penalties for their alleged mutineering.

After the uncle–nephew duo had served their prison sentence, their confiscated armour was returned to them. However, the Maharaja retained their release penalties and most of their confiscated lands, except one village each, which he handed back to them. Within eight days of their release, Thakur Bhopal Singhji and Durjan Singhji arrived at Mehrangarh to plead for Maharaja Man Singhji's mercies, to which the latter yielded. Kheenvsar and Panchodi were returned to them, and Thakur Bhopal Singhji was granted a homeward return in 1825. Barely a month after his release, he breathed his last.

13

Thakur Bakhtawar Singhji

The Maharaja's Attaché

Thakur Bhopal Singhji's sole consort, Umed Kanwar, was a Bhati princess from Bhikamkor. She birthed him a daughter, Naval Kanwar, and a son, Bakhtawar Singhji, who grew to become Kheenvsar's forthcoming ruler. Born in 1809, Bakhtawar Singhji was only 18 years old when his stately duties called upon him as Kheenvsar's 13th scion. He was granted the Maharaja's clearance to return to Kheenvsar the following year in 1829. Thakur Bakhtawar Singhji considered Maharaja Man Singhji a father figure and was granted the rare honour of leading the Maharaja's entourage on his stallion. Two letters soliciting Kheenvsar's presence, first at the Jodhpur durbar and second at a territorial dispute in Nagaur, have been recorded from Maharaja Man Singhji's desk.

Kheenvsar was a frequent attendee at Marwar's durbars, and Thakur Bakhtawar Singhji was even solicited to partake in the welcome ceremony for Lieutenant Colonel J. Sutherland, an agent of the Governor General, and his assistant, Captain Ludlow, in Digri. Camping arrangements were made for the two officials in Jodhpur on the grounds between Raikabagh and Sojatiya Gate. Maharaja Man Singhji soon handed over his fort's administrative responsibilities to them to commence his long-awaited refuge at Maylabagh.

Tucking the heavy bunch of keys handed over to him, Colonel Sutherland was walking past Mehrangarh's Surajpol when he was ambushed by a parole officer. Luckily for the Colonel, a guard stationed nearby counter-attacked and rescued him before he was injured. The assailant turned out to be a Karamsot Rathore from the Bhatnokha village and succumbed to his injuries five days later. This incident conveys a degree of reluctance towards colonialism on Marwar's part during the initial stages of British colonialism.

The onset of imperial rule notwithstanding, Kheenvsar enjoyed the rank of a sirayat until Maharaja Takhat Singhji assumed supreme charge over Marwar. Continued pillaging of Kheenvsar's peripheral settlements during Maharaja Man Singhji's time contributed to the souring of relations between Marwar and Kheenvsar.

In the absence of a successor, Maharaja Man Singhji expressed his dying wish to adopt Idar's prince, Takhat Singhji. After he was no more, his loyal chieftains ensured that their beloved Maharaja's command was fulfilled. In 1843, Marwar greeted Takhat Singhji with an elaborate welcome at Mogda and coronated him at Mehrangarh's Srinagar Chowk in 1843. Thakur Bakhtawar Singhji was present on both occasions and vowed his allegiance to Marwar's new Maharaja. In return, Maharaja Takhat Singhji honoured Kheenvsar's Thakur with a ceremonial turban.

Without any apparent rift between the two, Kheenvsar's exclusion from Maharaja Takhat Singhji's favoured list of chieftains remains a mystery, especially because Thakur Bakhtawar Singhji was summoned by the new Maharaja within a year of his enthronement to partake in a secret chamber in the middle of the night.

Kheenvsar's ambiguous rank as a sirayat was contested time and again by Thakur Bakhtawar Singhji and his kindred to no avail. In the time of H.H. Maharaja Gaj Singhji II, Kheenvsar was finally accorded recognition as a sirayat. This is elaborated upon in Chapter 18.

Thakur Bakhtawar Singhji died in 1848, and no other significant details about his life have been documented. He was survived by three sons, two from his first wife, Amaan Kunwar Bhati of Malunga, and one from his second, Naval Kunwar Chauhan of Sankhwas. His eldest son, Shivnath Singhji, assumed office at the age of eighteen.

14

Thakur Shivnath Singhji

Marwar's Close Aide

Thakur Shivnath Singhji became Kheenvsar's supremo in 1848 under the aegis of Jodhpur's

Maharaja Takhat Singhji. Given their lukewarm relations, Kheenvsar received the Maharaja's condolences for Thakur Bakhtawar Singhji four years after his passing. During a campaign in Pali, Maharaja Takhat Singhji made his way to Thakur Shivnath Singhji and paid his belated respects.

In the interim, the latter was presented with a turban on behalf of Marwar as per standard customs, indicating the Maharaja's approval of his succession. This prerogative was reserved for the select few chieftains whose familial condolences the Maharaja graced in person, which indicates Kheenvsar's enduring superiority in Marwar's ranks.

Thakur Shivnath Singhji was among Maharaja Takhat Singhji's closest aides and assisted him during most royal summons of political strategy and statecraft. He even constituted the administration that drafted as many as 23 new constitutional clauses for Marwar. A few of these included the right of access to the royal court for all workers and the right of princely states to receive official state alimonies upon the bereavement of their ruler.

Only once, when the Thakur made an unannounced visit to parlay with the Maharaja in Jodhpur, did he return empty-handed. The drafting body of thakurs presented their bills for mediation via the resident officers of the Rajputana Agency, Sir John Malcolm and Captain E.I. Hardcastle.

The Rajputana Agency was an official body formed by the British Indian Empire in 1832 CE; it was given the political charge of administering Rajputana and reporting directly to the Governor General. The colonial officers submitted these documents for the Maharaja to review, who failed to provide any official response despite receiving frequent reminders. Thus, the constitutional amendments that the Rajput administrators had painstakingly drafted faded away, and their potential for progress was halted.

Royal Alliances

In 1852, Maharaja Takhat Singhji visited the shrine of Char Bhujnath during his homeward journey after visiting his in-laws in Sirohi. A letter arrived from Jaipur, signed by Zorawar Pancholi, a Jodhpur-based officer. Herein, the Sawai's decision to soon make a nuptial departure for Rewa state was conveyed. Maharaja Takhat Singhji was nonplussed upon hearing this news because Sawai Ram Singhji of Jaipur was already engaged to be wed to Jodhpur's princess. Thakurs from Raas, Kuchaman, Aasop and Kheenvsar appeared before the Maharaja to devise a solution to the matter that had put Jodhpur's honour at stake. Thakur Shivnath Singhji and his fellow dignitaries assured their king of a timely intervention and ensured that Jaipur's wedding procession reached Jodhpur's doorstep before proceeding to Rewa Rewa.

Marwar gave away its daughter to Jaipur with much pomp and glamour. Adorned with lights as infinite as the stars above, Mehrangarh mirrored its royal bride in a splendid appearance that left everyone in awe. Kheenvsar's Thakur played a cardinal role in securing this significant wedlock.

The 1857 Freedom Revolution

Then arrived the monumental year of 1857, when a group of Indian sepoys of the East India Company's army rebelled against the British in Meerut. Rumour had it that the cartridges for the newly introduced Enfield rifle were greased with beef tallow and pork lard. To open the cartridge, its top had to be bitten off. This gravely offended the religious sentiments of Hindu and Muslim infantrymen and sparked a mutiny that spread like wildfire across Central India and the Upper Gangetic Plain. Iconic leaders such as Tatya Tope, Rani Lakshmibai, Begum Hazrat Mahal and Bahadur Shah Zafar had joined the revolutionary fray out of their shared contempt for the British. Tiny splinters from the revolution barely made their way into Marwar and just grazed past Nasirabad, Auwa and Pali.

Unlike the *Purbiya* Rajputs from Oudh and Bihar, most of Marwar's rulers remained supportive of the British during the 1857 freedom revolution. Auwa's Thakur Kushal Singhji defied Maharaja Takhat Singhji's orders and joined the freedom struggle but was subdued by the British forces, who besieged the fort at Auwa.

Fearing that anti-colonial sentiments would make their way into mainstream conscience in Rajputana, Maharaja Takhat Singhji engaged in several conferences with his chieftains. Amidst these congregations, an iconic meeting was held in Mehrangarh's Phool Mahal in 1858, but the session's minutes weren't brought to light. Bikaner's Maharaja Sardar Singhji is recorded as the sole ruler from Rajputana to command his forces to suppress the revolt.

Marwar's limited participation in the 1857 revolution, coupled with its silence during Bahadur Shah's execution, conveys its pro-British sentiment to compelling extents. Maharaja Takhat Singhji celebrated Britain's official acquisition of India by lighting up Mehrangarh and parts of Jodhpur with festive lamps.

For his loyalty towards the British rule in India, Jodhpur's Maharaja was granted a *sanad* of adoption. Sanads were deeds granted by the British to Indian rulers after the Indian War of Independence in 1857. By means of this deed, the bearer of the sanad could supersede the Doctrine of Lapse and adopt a chosen heir in case they lacked a direct successor.

When news of the Government of India Act, 1858, reached Maharaja Takhat Singhji, he rewarded the letter's bearer with many gifts. Whether Marwar responded out of complacency or prudent realism remains open to interpretation.

The Quelling of Another Rebellion

Maharaja Takhat Singhji continued seeking Thakur Shivnath Singhji's stately contributions. When Mundwa became the target of Barothiya dacoity, Kheenvsar's Thakur was called upon for assistance. Later, when the Maharaja's second son, Zorawar Singhji, contested for Marwar's throne and laid siege to Nagaur, Jodhpur's loyal sentinels came to its defence. They admonished the rebelling prince and his supporters from Khatu, Harsolav and Aanguta, and sent Zorawar Singhji in penance to Ajmer. Maharaja Takhat Singhji witnessed this ordeal from a distance because his duty called upon him to attend to Marwar's hinterlands.

During his return to Jodhpur, the Maharaja halted at Kheenvsar for a meal and refreshments. Thakur Shivnath Singhji ensured that each one of the Maharaja's chaperones was well fed and thoroughly looked after. Kheenvsar's hospitality delighted Maharaja Takhat Singhji and his men, and Thakur Shivnath Singhji was showered with jewels and costumes. As a parting gift, Kheenvsar's Thakur presented Jodhpur with two horses and two elephants. The female elephant was named Phoolmaal, and she was to be fed only the finest fodder and produce fortified with ghee, spices and lentil nuggets as per the Maharaja's royal orders.

Unpopular Tax Reforms

By the 1870s, Maharaja Takhat Singhji's views towards Kheenvsar changed. The system of revenue collection was mismanaged in ways that weighed heavily on state treasuries. Instead of an annual collection, revenues were to be paid cumulatively over four years. This revision called for more taxes to be collected from the citizens and received large-scale public disapproval. Because the thakurs were to ensure the timely collection of taxes, they became the objects of scorn.

Thakur Shivnath Singhji was no exception to disdain, and several of his merchants had defaulted on their payment of taxes. To avoid future delays in tax collection, he announced prison sentences for errant taxpayers. Two traders, namely, Prabhulal Bhatad and Amarchand Nadar, faced imprisonment, and their family members were detained until the accused cleared their dues. The aggrieved families of these merchants complained to the

Maharaja's court in Jodhpur and successfully obtained his orders for Thakur Shivnath Singhji's tax penalties to be reversed with immediate effect. A judicial officer from Nagaur was assigned to ensure the Thakur's compliance in favour of the mercantile community.

Maharaja Jaswant Singhji II

Public discord continued to fester even after Thakur Shivnath Singhji's orders had been revoked. The discontent simmered after Maharaja Takhat Singhji's death in 1873. Jodhpur's new Maharaja, Jaswant Singhji II, held a more pragmatic outlook towards the various concerns plaguing Marwar. For one, he enforced a strict system of surveillance over miscreants in the region. Reporting crimes and misdemeanours had now become a federal responsibility of the jagirs. Due to this revision, Maharaja Jaswant Singhji II enabled his secret services to keep a closer eye on potential fugitives.

Shortly after his coronation, Maharaja Jaswant Singhji II departed for a pilgrimage to Haridwar. Shortly after returning to Jodhpur in 1872, Marwar hosted agent Henry Walter, who surveyed the area for the census of India. Conducted during the rule of Viceroy Lord Mayo in 1872, this marked the first all-India census. Thakur Shivnath Singhji assembled with the Maharaja's other chieftains to extend Walter a warm welcome when he arrived in Jodhpur. In 1875, Maharaja Jaswant Singhji II was awarded the Knight Grand Commander of the Most Exalted Order of the Star of India by the British on behalf of Queen Victoria.

Maharaja Jaswant Singhji II by Narsingh

It is possible that Thakur Shivnath Singhji was still in service when he passed away in 1875 because he was residing in Jodhpur at the time. His funeral rites were conducted at the city's Kaga mortuary, and Maharaja Jaswant Singhji II expressed his deep grief at the death of his trusted chieftain.

Thakur Shivnath Singhji's legacy lived on through his widow Saroop Kanwar Chundawat of Kosithal (present-day Bhilwara) and their two children. His daughter, Mehtab Kanwar, born in 1852, was wedded to the Thakur of Chomu at the age of 12 years. Their son was birthed in 1857 and was on the brink of adulthood when he assumed office as Kheenvsar's 14th thakur.

15

Thakur Shardul Singhji

The Third King at Eighteen

Thakur Shardul Singhji shared a destiny similar to that of his father and grandfather, in that he too was coronated at the age of eighteen. Maharaja Jaswant Singhji II arrived at Kheenvsar's haveli to mourn the heavenly departure of late Thakur Shivnath Singhji within a year of his passing. He conducted all the customary rites prior to Thakur Shardul Singhji's coronation, including the ceremony of placing a coloured turban on the young Thakur's head.

Kheenvsar continued wielding prominence in Marwar's myriad affairs of state importance, such as festivities and royal councils. In 1882, Jodhpur requested the presence of 31 prime chieftains to rejoice in the betrothal of its princess. Kheenvsar was among them, and its status as Marwar's prime jagir gained elevation during the reign of Maharaja Jaswant Singhji II.

Abundant evidence of its primary status during the latter's reign is found in the Marwar Gazette.

Maharaja Jaswant Singhji II ordered the reorganization of seating protocols, whereby eight new jagirs, including that of Bhadrajun, were added to the list. Kheenvsar was amongst the four major jagirs to be eliminated from the ranks. Kheenvsar appealed for its status as a sirayat to be restored, but the imperial decision lay frozen in a political impasse.

Court of Sardars

Maharaja Jaswant Singhji II grew increasingly popular for restoring harmony between the jagirdars and judicial courts of Marwar. Until then, the jagirdars had long protested against several measures of jurisprudence that they deemed unreasonable. To their discredit, they found their stature being questioned by the civil and military courts of justice. Similarly, the tribunals accused most jagirdars of judicial breaches.

This gap was effectively bridged once Maharaja Jaswant Singhji formed a special advisory body called the Court of Sardars in July 1882.[1] It dealt with appellate jurisdiction in all civil cases concerning Rajput jagirs. It was made up of seven *sardars* chosen by the Maharaja, namely, Pokhran, Kuchaman, Nimaj, Aasop, Raipur, Khairwa and Riyan. Initially, this body provided immense relief to judicial stalemates and sped up the process of grievance redressal. However, within 13 months, the council proved to be disorderly and was dissolved.[2]

Although Kheenvsar wasn't involved in this perfunctory body, its thakur was granted the right to appoint its police force and judiciary council. Thakur Shardul Singhji was vested with the power of announcing prison sentences that spanned up to six months.

In 1895, Marwar observed state mourning for Maharaja Jaswant Singhji II, with chieftains such as Thakur Shardul Singhji observing austere practices of lamentation for their beloved ruler. Among its most popular rulers, Jaswant Singhji II also bears the credit of introducing telegraphs and railways to Marwar.[3] His successor, Maharaja Sardar Singhji, commissioned a white marble memorial known as Jaswant Thada to immortalize his greatness.

Jaswant Thada with Mehrangarh in the backdrop; Courtesy of Mehrangarh Museum Trust

His loyal men spent all their days and nights in the stable where the Maharaja's corpse rested prior to its cremation. Kheenvsar's Thakur journeyed homeward only after Marwar had observed every funeral rite. In the year after Maharaja Jaswant Singhji II's passing, Thakur Shardul Singhji followed him.

He left behind three widows and five children. His oldest son, Ranjit Singhji, inherited his title as a little child of 12. His mother, Thakurani Bakhtawar Kanwar Chauhan from Barmer's Kalyanpur, was the late Thakur's third wife and bore him his remaining four children. In the absence of their Thakur, his three Thakuranis diligently raised Ranjit Singhji and his siblings until they were old enough to uphold their ancestral legacy of glory.

16

Thakur Ranjit Singhji

The Fortifier

Thakur Ranjit Singhji wasn't fated to live the life of an ordinary teenager. In 1897, he entered his teens by assuming supreme command over Kheenvsar and taking a bride. Meja's Gulab Kanwar Sisodia is believed to have been a minor, too, when she became the Thakurani of Kheenvsar. Until the young Thakur became fit to assume matters of stately importance, a temporary advisory body was set up to govern Kheenvsar. In the absence of a male custodian, the Thakur of Danvra chaired this body and deployed his trusted men to carry out Kheenvsar's day-to-day affairs.

As per Kheenvsar's archives, Thakur Ranjit Singhji was sent to be educated at Ajmer's Mayo College shortly after his wedding. In subsequent letters he dispatched to his mother from school, Thakur Ranjit Singhji expressed acute homesickness and his general disinterest in the school's academic curriculum. He even pleaded to be brought back home and took several leaves to spend more time in Kheenvsar. His brother-in-law from Meja is said to have addressed him a letter around the same time, consoling him and asking him to remain strong after his father's demise.

Nine years later, a letter written to Meja by Ajmer's Dhonkal Singhji Rathore reveals the weddings of both Karamsot princesses, Anand Kanwar Baisa to Padampura and Aas Kanwar Baisa to Chomu, in the summer of 1908. Thakur Ranjit Singhji revelled in the celebrations, and Kheenvsar wed both its daughters in much pomp and style. Jodhpur displayed its keen participation by sending the Maharaja's royal elephant, saddle, palanquin, lodging camps and seating for the wedding party.

Despite his lack of scholarly acumen, Thakur Ranjit Singhji expressed a sincere interest in matters of statecraft. In a letter to his guardian, the Thakur Sahib of Danvra, he expresses hostility towards his paternal uncle, Sayabdanji, for his ill behaviour. Because he also resided in Kheenvsar's fort premises, their frequent quarrels made it arduous for the uncle–nephew duo to coexist.

Thakur Ranjit Singhji devised a solution whereby he relegated Sayabdanji to a *rawla* in the fort's immediate vicinity. Even though he resented his uncle, he found it appropriate to summon Sayabdanji's son, Sajjan Singhji, and bade him a deferential farewell with due arrangements to resettle in his newly designated premises.

When it came to fortifying Kheenvsar's borders, Thakur Ranjit Singhji spearheaded an offensive against Aasop and held one of its servants in captivity. After its initial resistance, Aasop retreated and lodged a complaint in the military court. The verdict was in Aasop's favour, and a band of 50 men were sent to capture Thakur Ranjit Singhji in Kheenvsar. They were ordered to bring him to his ancestral haveli in Jodhpur, where he remained under house arrest.

In 1910, when he was still under house arrest at the Kheenvsar haveli, Thakur Ranjit Singhji passed away at the young age of 24. He was succeeded by his two children. His daughter, Baisa Jaman Kanwar, was wed to Thakur Kalyan Singhji of Mehru, and his son, Kunwar Kesri Singhji, was only eight years old when the world mourned the loss of his father.

17

Thakur Kesri Singhji

The Roaring Karamsot Lion

Born in 1901, Thakur Kesri Singhji wasn't even 9 years old when he took charge as Kheenvsar's new thakur. Despite being a minor, Kheenvsar's custodianship wasn't put under the temporary charge of an alternative jagirdar. This was contrary to the standard practice, which relegated a minor's thikana to a suitable ward till the regent came of age. Marwar's exceptional accordance of Kheenvsar to its minor Thakur can be explained by the high stature held by the Karamsots.

Like his father, Thakur Kesri Singhji was enrolled at Mayo College, where he flourished as an exceptional student. He not only exhibited academic brilliance but was also an ace sportsman and star wrestler. His all-round excellence in both academics and sports earned him the prestigious Prince of Wales Medal from King Edward VIII. Thakur Kesri Singhji graduated from Mayo College with flying colours as a college monitor with a first division.

Thakur Kesri Singhji with his staff: A portrait

Thakur Kesri Singhji and Maharaja Umaid Singhji of Jodhpur studied together at Mayo. Sharing deep camaraderie, the duo maintained close contact even after their Mayo days and held many meetings in Kheenvsar and Jodhpur. Thakur Kesri Singhji seldom missed Jodhpur durbar's various official gatherings, be it during the Akha Teej in 1928 or Lord Northbrook's viceregal tour in 1932. He is said to have spent most of his time between 1937 and 1940 in Jodhpur and was the Maharaja's chosen chieftain to receive Marwar's *baijilal* in Jaipur. The Karamsot Thakur even accompanied Maharaja Umaid Singhji as his duty officer to receive his widowed sister, Majisahib Chauhanji, at Raikabagh in the winter of 1937.

The following year, the Maharaja summoned a special gathering of his chieftains and brethren wherein he, his chief minister and Maharaj Kumar Ajit Singhji delivered speeches. Thakur Kesri Singhji was present at this summit at Raikabagh Palace, and most of the attending dignitaries happened to be chief contributors to the treasuries for World Wars I and II.

Kheenvsar's status among Marwar's primary tier of sirayats was made all the more palpable by its independent police authority. However, this situation soon changed. By 1940, mounting land taxes had escalated tensions between Marwar's farmers and jagirdars to an all-time high. Maharaja Umaid Singhji set up the Lag Bag Committee to comprehensively review the tax system levied on the farmers with the hopes of improving their incomes. Thakur Kesri Singhji was appointed as Nagaur's official representative.

From Friends to Foes

When World War II was in full swing, some farmers from Kheenvsar's Tadas and Zorawarpura villages filed complaints against their state officials on more than five occasions. Their advocate dispatched letters to the Nagaur government office and the Chief Minister's secretariat. Historians assume a falsity in these farmers' claims and argue that had such public grievances been genuine, similar complaints would have arisen out of the remaining 17 villages as well. In actuality, the primary factor that fuelled Jat farmer agitations was the state's alleged tax collection in the form of food grains. Agrarian dissent accumulated and cascaded into a larger anti-establishment movement.

When farmer agitations gained momentum, several jagirdars arrived at Thakur Kesri Singhji's doorstep with a negotiatory bid in 1944. This cohort was primarily motivated against the recently announced arms act, which reduced the number of arms permissible to official license bearers.

Owing to their Kshatriya heritage, the majority of Rajputs were entitled to a rich inheritance of weapons and armour. Apart from being considered precious family heirlooms, they were also objects of worship. Every year during Dussehra, the Rajput custom of *shastra puja* called for the veneration of weaponry and armour, and the new act curtailed the right to basic arms possession amongst the Rajputs.

The jagirdars who had come seeking Thakur Kesri Singhji's support were well aware of his enduring connections with the Maharaja since their school days.

Kheenvsar's Thakur concurred with the validity of this plea and sent numerous requests for the Maharaja's review. Instead of viewing the matter through the lens of civil discord, Maharaja Umaid Singhji snubbed his contemporary in Kheenvsar. An earnest plea from Kheenvsar on an issue of religious sentimentality ended up being misjudged by the Maharaja as an audacious act of rebellion directed to humiliate him.

In return, the Jodhpur durbar exerted regal disapproval with such force that every appellant, except Thakur Kesri Singhji, stepped back. He refused to back down and persevered with his plea, irrespective of the consequences doing so would bring upon Kheenvsar.

When Maharaja Umaid Singhji began to ascertain Kheenvsar's steadfastness, he severed his relationship with Thakur Kesri Singhji. From being a close childhood friend, Maharaja Umaid Singhji began to look down upon Kheenvsar's Thakur as a rebel. This hostility manifested in Jodhpur's relegation of Kheenvsar under the Court of Wards, thereby ceasing Thakur Kesri Singhji's erstwhile sovereignty.

As per the Court of Wards Act 1879, British law placed the charge of a ruler-less or disputed property under the charge of a guardian or ward appointed by the royal court. Thakur Kesri Singhji criticized the stringent measure as one that was highly uncalled for because his opposition was by no means directed at the Maharaja but at a state policy. Moreover, Thakur Kesri Singhji protested for Kheenvsar's status as a sirayat to be restored, but Marwar implied otherwise.

The distressed Thakur of Kheenvsar appealed for the intervention of Jodhpur's Chief Minister, D.M. Field, by writing him a letter. Thereafter, he received a letter from the governor of Nagaur in which he had been summoned to Jodhpur on behalf of Maharaja Umaid Singhji.

Thakur Kesri Singhji readily agreed to appear before D.M. Field but had felt upset at being solicited indirectly through a state orderly despite his long-standing friendship with the Maharaja. More importantly, this act amounted to a breach of protocol considering Kheenvsar's exalted rank amongst Marwar's states, which called for direct correspondence as opposed to mediated messages.

Thakur Bakhtawar Singhji Rathore, the then Deputy Inspector-General of Police, Jodhpur State, made an official visit to Kheenvsar to negotiate with Thakur Kesri Singhji on the Maharaja's behalf. After two full days of discussion with the Thakur, he returned to Jodhpur on the orders of the revenue minister.

Thakur Kesri Singhji maintained personal journals, which contain his ruminations on the precarity of these affairs. He writes, 'I am unable to fathom how a meeting with the chief minister has allegedly been converted into a meeting with the revenue minister. I wonder what it is that the state's head officials have in mind.'

Come September, another visitor met Thakur Kesri Singhji in Kheenvsar. This time, it was the Thakur of Pal, another bearer of the Maharaja's message summoning him to Jodhpur. The former succeeded in coaxing Thakur Kesri Singhji to present himself before the Maharaja, but he did so only after seeking an ordinance with Maharaj Kumar Ajit Singhji in his dwelling. He delivered a thorough account of the recent events to the young prince who, in turn, assured that he would convey his words to the Maharaja.

Ajit Singhji also urged the Karamsot Thakur to maintain cordiality during his negotiations with the concerned authorities and arranged for a vehicle from the royal garage to drive him back to Kheenvsar. He, along with the thakurs of Pal and Aasop, were delegated the responsibility of sounding off several Rajput chieftains about the Maharaja's newly-ordered cartography exercises across Marwar, which would delineate several borders that seemed to remain unclear thus far. Thakur Kesri Singhji returned to Jodhpur the same day after performing his duties. He also heeded Maharaj Kumar Ajit Singhji's advice of sending the detailed minutes of these to the revenue minister. A subsequent letter was penned by Thakur Kesri Singhji on 3 October 1944 for the revenue minister, but he received no reply.

An Era of Detention

Around the same time, surveys for the impending land settlements were taking place in full swing. Thakur Kesri Singhji felt snubbed by the Maharaja and was disheartened by this treatment. He had recently fulfilled the duties ordered upon him by the Maharaja, but his efforts remained unreciprocated. The last straw came in the form of a letter from D.M. Fields, which revealed the Maharaja's orders to detain Thakur Kesari Singhji in Jodhpur until further notice.

Even when adversity stared Thakur Kesri Singhji in the face, he expressed a range of emotions. On the one hand, he praised Maharaja Umaid Singhji for cancelling the infamous arms act and adhered to his detention orders. On the other hand, he criticized various state officials for their contemptuous behaviour towards him and denounced the contradictions in the Maharaja's arms reforms, which continued imposing licenses on British guns.

Despite the Karamsot Thakur's forewarnings, Maharaja Umaid Singhji chose to place his trust in petty state officials over his own blood. As per the royal orders published in the Rajasthan Gazette, all of Kheenvsar's judiciary and police authorities were to be seized by Marwar. Crestfallen, Thakur Kesri Singhji lamented the Maharaja's lack of judgement in a letter dated 18 March 1945, 'I am beyond disheartened that Maharaja Sahib mistook my opposition against his state policies as a personal assault and rendered me a rebel. I am unable to comprehend the reason for my punishments and the royal wrath that has descended upon me. Nevertheless, I swear allegiance to Maharaja Umaid Singhji and pronounce my undying loyalty to Marwar even under a state of arrest. I only ask the durbar to fulfil one last wish of mine: please bless my son.'

An editorial in the weekly newspaper, *Hindu Haridwar*, dated 9 January 1945, highlighted inferences of vicious propaganda that often evaded the Maharaja's notice. It can be translated as follows:

> Jodhpur's thikanas, Kheenvsar, Phalodi, Chandawal, Bagri, Sihar, etc., too are reporting incidents of Rajput jagirdars being systemically overthrown by their rebellious adversaries in a political conspiracy that is being augmented fully by the national press. News of selective oppositions against

> these states are being exaggerated and amplified via several daily newspapers of Delhi. Thus, it is imperative for the governments of Jaipur and Jodhpur to take immediate action against the perpetrators of these disturbances. Any delay in their undertaking of corrective action is likely to disrupt the peace and harmony of these sirayats, and a united protest of this nature will prove to be detrimental to the society. Jagirdars and thikanedars are the true loyalists and well-wishers of their Maharajas, and any falsified protests against them must be extinguished as the utmost need of the hour.

The Court of Wards

Amidst these tumultuous times, the exiled Thakur's only child, Kunwar Onkar Singhji, was a few months shy of his eighteenth birthday. Marwar capitalized on this miniscule detail to place Kheenvsar under the Court of Wards. As per its stipulations, Kunwar Onkar Singhji's maternal grandfather, Thakur Zorawar Singhji of Ghabana, was granted regency over Kheenvsar until 1949.

By the time Kunwar Onkar Singhji attained the legal age to assume his custodianship over Kheenvsar, India had attained independence and become a sovereign democratic republic.

All princely states were beginning to integrate into the Indian nation state, and Thakur Onkar Singhji was left with nothing but an ornamental title. As for Thakur Kesri Singhji, he continued to honour the Maharaja's wishes. In 1977, he suffered a cardiac arrest in Jaipur, which he didn't survive. He was 75 years old when he departed for the heavens on 7 March 1977.

Kheenvsar's Most Noble Karamsot

Despite his thwarted career as Kheenvsar's ruler and a prolonged souring of relations with Marwar, Thakur Kesri Singhji was far from a dull glimmer in Kheenvsar's glorious skies. On the contrary, he was among its brighter stars. To date, he is remembered for being the most principled man of his times.

A true noble, he was widely respected by Marwar's distinguished rulers. Thakur Kesri Singhji was the first elected Member of Legislative Assembly from Nagaur in independent India. He had contested as a member of the Ram Rajya Parishad Party that had the Maharaja of Jodhpur as the party president.

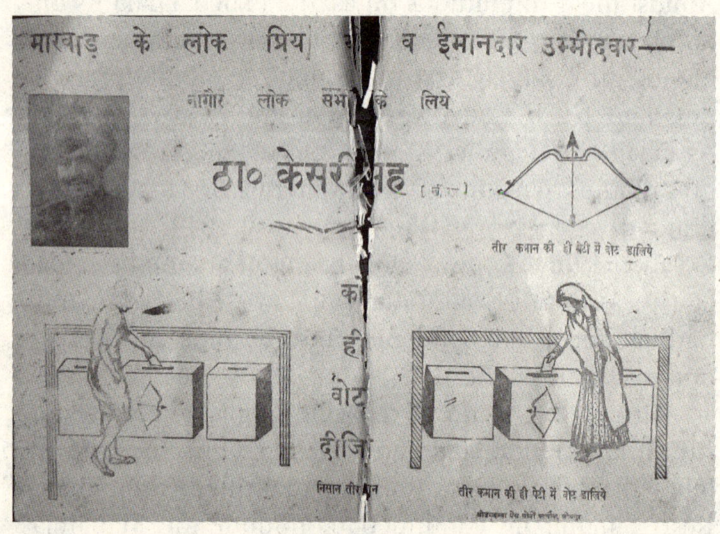

A leaflet encouraging the citizenry to vote for Thakur Kesri Singhji during election time

Owing to his rare brilliance, Thakur Kesri Singhji was shortlisted to receive military training from the esteemed Royal Military Academy at Sandhurst but was unable to avail of this opportunity due to Maharaja Umaid Singhji's decision to veto his selection.

Thakur Kesri Singhji is also remembered as an avid literarian and renowned historian. He maintained an elaborate in-house library that held the diverse works of Premchand, Tagore, Kanhaiyalal Maneklal Munshi, Jainendra Kumar, Durga Prasad Khatri, Ramchandra Tiwari and Suryakant Tripathi, among others, and had read his select favourites a dozen times over. He collected some rare historical archives and records with the help of the Maharaj Kumar of Sitamau and attempted to chronicle the history of the Karamsot Rathores. His love for prose, character study and even ghazals is well-known. He maintained as many as eight to ten diaries for journaling. In his later years, Thakur Kesri Singhji devoured the elaborate and suspenseful volumes of James Hadley Chase.

An ardent yogi, Thakur Kesri Singhji's day remained unfinished without his daily yoga ritual. He placed firm belief in indigenous medicinal remedies and admitted himself to ayurvedic institutes for months in pursuit of this fascination.

Once, when he was due to undergo cataract surgery, he refused to be anaesthetized, much to the horror of his ophthalmologist friend. After all, Kheenvsar's brave forefathers had lay severed in battles far and near, and they would consider it a shame if their son failed to bear the slight pains in his eye.

During Thakur Kesri Singhji's times, the moat

surrounding Kheenvsar's fort held fierce wild boars with big tusks. He found that breeding boars served two purposes. One, the boars offered protective vigilance against intruders, and two, they helped fulfil Thakur Sahib's hobby of pig-sticking. This age-old sport had spear-armed players mounted on their steeds, following which a ferocious wild boar was set loose. Thakur Sahib and his horse-mounted team would then hunt down the boar for the evening's supper feast. A miss and the murderous boar would tear apart the horse and its spear-holding rider.

The brave and bold scion of Kheenvsar was famous for his tent-pegging and hunting skills. Even at the age of 70, he shot a sprinting hare with his 12-bore shotgun. His grandson, Raja Gajendra Singhji, fondly recalls this memory as an awestruck spectator. This transgenerational bond between grandfather and grandson thrived till the end of Thakur Sahib's days. His grandson, whom he affectionately referred to as Gajju, was the apple of his eye. Gajju lived and slept in Thakur Sahib's room. As a young child, he remembers having to exhibit discipline and hard work even for a bar of chocolate. In his grandfather or Annadata's words, 'You had to earn it.' The coincidence of Bourneville's tagline, 'cannot be bought, it must be earned,' is an uncanny reverberation of the grand old Thakur Sahib's lesson.

Much as he was driven by morals and gusto, the Thakur didn't lack a funny bone. He was a formidable wrestler and thoroughly enjoyed watching wrestling bouts. Every time a contesting *pehelwan* pinned the loser flat on his back, he'd roar with laughter till he had tears trickling down his cheeks.

Thakur Kesri Singhji was a dashing young man of nineteen when he married Ghabana's Rajendra Kunwar Jadon. Together, they were blessed with one child, Thakur Onkar Singhji, heir to Kheenvsar. Thakur Sahib appointed two guardians who bore the singular responsibility of keeping a watch on their son around the clock. They were also to ensure that he was fed a nutritious diet of nuts and grains.

A farmer, Shankar Gehlot, and his son, Roop Singh Gehlot, recalled Kheenvsar in the era of Thakur Kesri Singhji as they tilled their fields near the fort's Fateh Mahal. They express much praise for his administration and report the tentative strength of 100–150 people that served as Kheenvsar's employees during his time. Roop Singh Gehlot recalls Kheenvsar's breeding of cows, cattle, pigs and around 40 horses and 40 camels in Thakur Kesri Singhji's stables. Even Kheenvsar's jail premises accorded its convicts the dignity of segregation between male and female prisoners, who were guarded by 12 sepoys and one senior supervisor.

Overall, Thakur Kesri Singhji's reign over Kheenvsar facilitated progress, development and a harmonious populace. However, one point of contention lay unresolved throughout his life. It was regarding the political impasse over Kheenvsar's rightful status as Marwar's sirayat. This enduring ambiguity persisted from the Mughal era through British rule and into independent India. From the late H.H. Maharaja Man Singhji to the incumbent H.H. Maharaja Umaid Singhji, no Marwar ruler was fully able to restore Kheenvsar's glory with its original status as a sirayat, and with every subsequent generation, this chasm only widened.

18

Raja Onkar Singhji and Rani Sneh Lata

The Modern Statesman and a Kashmiri Princess

Early Years

At first, his parents named Raja Onkar Singhji Akhyaraj, but once he grew up, his astrological beliefs and superstitions caused him to change his name to Onkar. Born as Kheenvsar's only child in his generation, Raja Onkar Singhji enjoyed a highly protected childhood, receiving everyone's undivided love and attention.

When Marwar imposed the Court of Wards on Kheenvsar out of personal vendetta, Raja Onkar Singhji was 4 months shy of his eighteenth birthday. So close and yet so far, Jodhpur used the marginal gap of four months as justification for Kheenvsar's custodianship being passed to Ghabana.

In the meantime, Raja Onkar Singhji pursued his education at the Doon School as well as Mayo College. He then pursued a law degree at the University of Lucknow, where he achieved a second division. In 1949, he penned a letter to Maharaja Umaid Singhji, informing him of his return to Kheenvsar. Thakur Kesri Singhji had earlier abdicated his seat as Kheenvsar's Thakur at the Maharaja's behest; hence, his son was granted the nominal title sans revenue and judicial authorities now that India was an independent nation.

Raja Onkar Singhji followed suit in his appeal to reinstate Kheenvsar's status as a sirayat. As per protocol, the durbar seated Rao Jodha's brothers, sons and their families on both sides of the Maharaja. Sawai Raja Sur Singhji had amended this court etiquette in 1595 and accorded the sirayat status to the estates of eight jagirdars. Kheenvsar had been included in this list of eight until Maharaja Takhat Singhji increased the number to twelve and excluded Kheenvsar from this list. Despite numerous appeals from Thakur Kesri Singhji and Raja Onkar Singhji, no favourable decision could be secured from the centre. Eventually, this entire issue was made redundant when Marwar acceded to the Indian republic.

That said, Raja Onkar Singhji was authorized to maintain his sub-jurisdiction within the four walls of Kheenvsar Fort. It is believed that by this time, the revenue and judicial rights of jagirdars had been abolished. Jagirdars who had wielded judicial rights up to this point were permitted to retain a *phaatak*, which had a dual meaning. One meaning referred to their right to construct a wall and insert a gate for common thoroughfare. The other referred to their right to retain a prison gate. This trend popularly came to be referred to as the phaatak system, but it was abolished in 1949 with then Chief Minister Nathuram Mirdha's announcement.[1] The revenue powers of all jagirdars had been revoked as per official orders only a week prior.

Kheenvsar's ongoing renovation works were placed under the young Raja's supervision. According to a letter written by Kunwar Tej Singhji to the treasurer on 6 April 1949, construction work had been completed till the third level.[2] Raja Onkar Singhji is said to have been dedicatedly raised under his father's guidance, and his upbringing was deeply inculcated with Indian values. He was initiated into military training at a young age and expressed keen interest in it, as he did in horse riding and sharpshooting. Raja Onkar Singhji was eager to grasp the know-how of politics, governance and international relations.

Nikheji: The Kashmiri Bride

Early Years

The youngest of three siblings, her family members affectionately called her Nikheji, meaning small one in Dogri. She had a turbulent childhood in Poonch, which was on the frontlines of India's dreadful partition. Poonch was embroiled in communal strife, and Kheenvsar's Majisab vividly recalled those dreadful times even as a nonagenarian.

Nikheji's father, the late Jagat Deo Singhji of Poonch, considered his youngest child his favourite. He had wished to raise her as the sitar maestro he could never be and even bought Nikheji a tiny sitar. As fate would have it, Poonch's Raja contracted typhoid and suffered an untimely death in 1940, leaving behind his widow and children. Nikheji was only 7 years old at the time.

Raja Jagat Deo Singhji of Poonch

The Annexation of Poonch

Kashmir's Maharaja Hari Singh seized this opportunity to annex the state of Poonch. The deceased king's sole heir, Shivratan Deo Singh, was still a minor, and under this pretext, the Maharaja began to annex Poonch. The widowed queen, Rani Padmavati Devi, put up a valiant fight against him until a much more judicial regent, Maharaja Dr Karan Singhji, took charge of Kashmir. By the time he stepped in, Poonch had lost its autonomy, and Maharaja Hari Singhji had acceded Kashmir to the Republic of India.

When her family moved to their haveli in Lahore, they kept vigil on many nights as the newly partitioned nations exchanged heaps of dead bodies in train carriages. To her ears, the ubiquitous cries of 'Jai Shri Ram' and 'Allahu Akbar' echoed an identical negation of humanity. Nikheji and her siblings had to wear poison-filled amulets around their necks to shield them from potential attacks or invasions. They were told that should an enemy break into their house, death by suicide was more honourable than being slaughtered by the enemy.

As a result of the Indo-Pakistani war (1947–1948), Poonch was severed into two halves. The western half was illegally occupied by Pakistan, whereas the eastern half was assimilated into the Rajouri Poonch district of the Indian state of Jammu and Kashmir. The entire Poonch kindred moved lock, stock and barrel to the pristine hill station of Dehradun for its thriving education hubs that could amply nourish the children. In the interim, the state took control over the Poonch Haveli, which is presently a neglected government building.

Carrying the sole literary skill of signing her name, which she was taught by her deceased husband, Poonch's widowed Rajmata Padmavati Devi raised her children single-handedly.[3] She became more pious with age and, at one point, only bathed with *gangajal.* Poonch House was situated on the main *ghats* of Haridwar's Har ki Pauri, where Rajmata Padmavati Devi stepped down into a private ghat for her daily bath.

Nikheji's Scholarly Dreams

Nikheji was an avid reader and a keen historian. She pleaded with her mother to send her for further studies, but no parent could risk their child's security in the stark shadows of a communally charged atmosphere. However, Rani Padmavati Devi was finding it increasingly difficult to resist her younger daughter's eager pleas. She relented on the sole condition that her older daughter would accompany her in the academic pursuit. Unlike Nikheji, Poonch's elder princess Vijaya detested studies and would often tear her sister's books to shreds, abruptly ending their scholarly pursuits. Nikheji refused to give this up, even if it meant being home tutored. Her mother's refusal to expose her to the outside world of academia was a grouse she held against her mother afterwards.

Nikheji accepted her fate and diverted her melancholy into reading Mirza Ghalib's poems, for which she pursued self-taught Urdu lessons with the help of her household staff. She soon discovered her talent for linguistics and mastered Urdu and several other languages, such as Nepalese, Punjabi, her native Dogri, and Marwari, after getting married.

Rani Sneh Lata: A portrait

Nuptial Ties with Kheenvsar

Nikheji's older sister was wed to a noble from the Himalayan state of Kunihar; her brother, Shivratan Singh Deo, married Princess Nalini Shah of Nepal.[4] When news of Kheenvsar's eminent bachelor reached her, Rajmata Padmavati Devi sent her *munshi* to inspect Nikheji's prospective *sasuraal*. She paid a handsome dowry to the Karamsots, which they used to construct the Onkar Niwas in Kheenvsar Fort. Cognizant of Poonch's erstwhile grandness, Raja Onkar Singhji ensured that Kheenvsar was well prepared to offer the Kashmiri princess a comfortable abode. What remained of the dowry helped fund his wedding.

After an overnight train journey, the newly-wed Kashmiri bride awoke to her first morning in Marwar and asked her accompanying Kashmiri maids to gather flowers for her daily *puja* rituals. She was surprised to see the maids return empty-handed, their eyes welling up with tears. When she asked them what the matter was, they pointed towards the window. Looking out, she found that till the horizon, there wasn't a single tree, let alone any flowers. A few *khejris* were all the foliage that Kheenvsar had the pleasure of knowing in those times.

Majisab Sneh Lata's Numerous Hats

Green Fingers

Now the consort of Kheenvsar's prince, she brought many waves of change. Upon a terrace in Kheenvsar Fort's *baradari* area, Majisab Sneh Lata grew her kitchen garden. She remembers being asked what the kitchen should prepare for her as a newlywed bride. When she uttered 'rice', the cook asked her what that was. Thereafter, Poonch's princess bears credit for introducing her beloved staple, rice, to the wheat and millet-eating household of Kheenvsar.

Devi Bhakti

Majisab Sneh Lata brought significant changes to Kheenvsar's observance of *Navratri* as well. Most Rajput households in Marwar celebrated Navratri by observing a day-long fast and sacrificing animals for the Navdurgas in the evening. Communal feasts and merriment with alcohol were common practices only until Majisab Sneh Lata stepped in. She converted the entire affair into a frugal and vegetarian one. A temporary kitchen was set up in her Devi's sanatorium every Navratri, where she would prepare *falhaari* meals. She spent all nine nights sleeping on a thin jute mat and her days in prayer.

Knitting behind a Ghoonghat

Being wed to Kheenvsar's only child came with its fair share of challenges. Her otherwise charitable and popular mother-in-law, Thakurani Rajendra Kumari of Ghabana, was a possessive mother to her son. She'd often taunt her daughter-in-law for hailing from a princely state of exalted stature, sidelining the princess's simplicity.

Thakur Kesri Singhji respected his daughter-in-law. The gentleman that he was, he believed in keeping his eyes downcast in the presence of any lady other than his wife. Customary to the traditions back then, Majisab Sneh Lata remembers always maintaining her veil around her father-in-law.

A particularly endearing story revolves around a sweater she knitted for Thakur Kesri Singhji. One day, the young bride decided to knit a sweater for her father-in-law, but there was a tiny problem. How could she dare to commit the act of measuring his size? A man who didn't dare cast his eyes upon her would most certainly decline allowing his measurements to be taken by his daughter-in-law. Caught in a predicament, Majisab Sneh Lata used her scholarly prowess. Though she preferred history over mathematics, she focused on calculating her father-in-law's shoulder width and the length of his torso using ratio. When he sat on the swing to read his newspaper, Majisab Sneh Lata would stand behind him to ascertain the ideal size for his sweater. To her delight, she succeeded in knitting a sweater that aptly fit Thakur Kesri Singhji.

Canines and Livestock

Majisab Sneh Lata loved dogs. Throughout her lifetime, she adopted many canines, most of them samoyeds that she christened Pinky, Dinky, Chinky, Brandy and Snowie. The last one was a Pekingese presented to her by Raja Onkar Singhji on one of her birthdays, whom she called Cookie.

In her middle age, Majisab Sneh Lata maintained a hen coop in Kheenvsar and several cows in Jaipur. Her daughter-in-law, Rani Priti Kumari, fondly recalls the comical sight of the time one of their cows had to be taken to the vet. 'The cow was loosely tied to the tail winch of our Mahindra jeep, and the driver was instructed not to exceed 10 kmph. The cow, with her jingling bell, leisurely tottered behind. It was a sight to behold,' she exclaims.

The World of Music and Literature

Given her strong affinity for Hindi and Urdu, Majisab Sneh Lata kept a sizeable collection of novels and magazines. In English, she opted for James Hadley Chase from her father-in-law's collection. It remained her constant companion. Just as she had feared all her life, Majisab Sneh Lata too battled hereditary dementia in her later years, much like her mother before her. In more lucid times, Kheenvsar's Majisab was a die-hard fan of Indian cricket, ghazals and Bollywood music. To our amazement, she could render the timeless melodies of Malika Pukhraj as deftly as the contemporary hits of Himesh Reshammiya and Mika Singh.

Majisab Sneh Lata lived past the age of ninety-two before succumbing to geriatric ailments. Chronic anaemia and COPD-related breathlessness led to her hospitalization, and after a 22-day-long battle in the private ICU of Jaipur's Santokba Durlabhji Memorial Hospital, the brave Dogra princess breathed her last on 5 September 2025. She was cremated at Padamsar in Kheenvsar the following day.

Aamchi Mumbai

Affectionately referred to by Raja Onkar Singhji as 'madam', she accompanied him through the best and worst of times. From braving many sandstorms during humbler times in Kheenvsar to travelling overseas, the charming duo shared a love for exploring the diversity of their world. Of all the exotic places his madam had visited, Raja Onkar Singhji knew that Bombay was her favourite. At a point, Majisab Sneh Lata became convinced that in a previous life, she had been a Mumbaikar. She romanticized the city's cosmopolitan pulse, its temperate climate, the vast expanse of the sea and the busy streets, so much so that Raja Onkar Singhji honoured her love for the city and bought her an apartment there. Together, they made long biannual trips to Maximum City.

Days of Motherhood and Aunthood

Majisab Sneh Lata is succeed by her two children. Her son, Raja Gajendra Singhji, was born on 25 December

1957 in Jodhpur. Seven years later, on 2 June, she gave birth to Baisa Sunita Kumari, whom she affectionately calls Kitty.

Apart from her own offspring, Majisab Sneh Lata also helped raise her brother's numerous children. Her sister-in-law, Princess Nalini, was known to have spent most of her life in Nepal, during which Majisab attended to her nieces and nephews. Among the five children was her oldest niece, Jodhpur's incumbent Maharani Sahiba Hemlata Raje. Thakur Onkar Singhji receives much credit for playing matchmaker for her wedding to Maharaja Gaj Singhji II.

Rajasthan's Forthcoming Administrator

Amidst the rapid waves of change that Rajasthan witnessed in his times, Raja Onkar Singhji maintained cordial relations with his region's prominent diplomats. He played an instrumental role in campaigning for his father during the country's first legislative assembly election in 1952; his father emerged victorious. The then magistrate of Rajasthan High Court, Indranath Modiji, specially invited Raja Onkar Singhji in 1955 for his daughter's wedding ceremony in Nagaur, and Kheenvsar's budding statesman graciously attended the illustrious gathering. This incident reveals Raja Onkar Singhji's prominence in Rajasthan's political arena.

Raja Onkar Singhji contested two legislative elections from Nawa but did not win. His continued attempts in the parliamentary elections as a Congress candidate from Nagaur and Barmer also proved to be futile. These tiny defeats did not dull his intrinsic spirit of statesmanship. A setback in the populist sphere of leadership hinted at a chance in the capital's central avenues. Thakur Onkar Singhji served Rajasthan through several administrative roles. He was made a director in the Rajasthan Pradesh Congress Committee and chairman of the Rajasthan State Finance Commission, Rajasthan Tourism Development Corporation and the State Tanneries.

His favourable image in Rajasthan's Congress Committee only multiplied over the years, and Thakur Onkar Singhji continued to be appointed and re-appointed at prestigious administrative offices. News of his diplomatic influence reached the Gandhi family, and he consolidated enduring goodwill with them. Over the decades, Raja Onkar Singhji remained an invaluable asset to the Congress party and influenced Nagaur's political climate in the party's favour.

During his era, Kheenvsar's fort was rebranded as Khimsar Fort. One of India's first heritage hotels, Khimsar Fort was in the vanguard of Rajasthan's booming heritage tourism industry. It was one of the first ancestral forts to be converted into a heritage hotel. Raja Onkar Singhji hosted then Prime Minister Indira Gandhi here. He was close friends with Rajasthan's former chief minister, Barkatullah Khan, who had appointed him as a deputy minister. Khan fondly referred to him as Duke.

On 7 March 1977, Raja Onkar Singhji lost his father and shouldered the entire weight of Kheenvsar's responsibilities. He consecrated his parents' cenotaphs at Padamsar, which were refurnished in 2008 by his successor, Gajendra Singhji.

On Raja Onkar Singhji's 80th birthday celebrations, Marwar's Maharaja Gaj Singhji II awarded him the title of Raja. The charitable Maharaja Gaj Singhji II had referred to Mehrangarh's archives to correctly deduce Kheenvsar's rightful rank of a sirayat. Given this stately status and Kheenvsar's unwavering loyalty to Marwar through every fateful war and tribulation, Maharaja Sahib graciously restored Kheenvsar's title from Thakur to Raja in Raja Onkar Singhji's lifetime.

Raja Onkar Singhji died in Jaipur two years later as a fulfilled and grand old man of 82. He had succumbed to cancer after battling several ailments for nearly two long decades. Majisab Sneh Lata was by his side all along as his foremost caretaker and support system. On the many occasions that he was wheeled in and out of hospitals in Mumbai and Jaipur, he never failed to make his doctors and nurses smile. Be it the head of a medical department or a humble janitor, Thakur Onkar Singhji's light-heartedness and undying sense of humour are cherished to date.

The spirited Thakur Sahib's legacy lives on through his son, Raja Gajendra Singhji, and daughter, Baisa Sunita Kumari, who was betrothed to Tirwa's Kunwar Shardul Narayan Singhji on 4 February 1985. They were blessed with two children, Bhanej Baisa Bhavini Singh and Bhanej Bana Trivikram Singh of Tirwa.

19

Raja Gajendra Singhji and Rani Priti Kumari

The People's Raja and Rani

It was a Christmas morning in 1957 when the newborn wails of a baby boy pierced through the jingling carols at

Jodhpur's Umaid Hospital. Because the nurses attending to Majisab Sneh Lata were Christians, they considered this birth auspicious. They inquired whether the mother might be considering giving up her baby, for he might be a reincarnation of Jesus. Shunning their excitement as best as she could, Majisab Sneh Lata celebrated the birth of her cherished baby boy. The Karamsots of Marwar rose in celebration to welcome Rao Karamsiji's 19th direct descendant and Kheenvsar's most exemplary torch bearer, Raja Gajendra Singhji.

Raja Gajendra Singhji spent much of his childhood under his grandfather's doting eyes. Thakur Kesri Singhji's life began to revolve around his little grandson, who was mischievous and innocent in competing measures. Raja Gajendra Singhji credits his beloved Annadata for instilling in him the virtues that shaped him into the man he is today.

For example, when the little boy began to develop a sweet tooth, his grandfather taught him the value of earning a treat with good deeds and service. Gajju, as he was affectionately known, learned to cherish life's smallest pleasures, be it a bar of chocolate or the carefree days of his childhood.

Raja Gajendra Singhji was only five years old when his parents sent him to Welham Prep in Dehradun. Thakur Kesri Singhji bore the heaviest heart seeing his little boy go. Even as a 68-year-old, he vividly recollects his grandfather parking his jeep near the railway crossing next to their Civil Lines residence in Jaipur with their Samoyed, Sandy, perched atop the vehicle's bonnet. Each time he made his journey back to school, the two would wait for their Gajju's carriage to chug past them.

When it did, he'd find them waving at him one last time before the engine gathered momentum towards the Doon Valley. Their bond only strengthened over time, from Thakur Kesri Singhji as his forthright guardian to becoming his best friend when Raja Gajendra Singhji grew into a young man.

Raja Gajendra Singhji pursued his early education at Dehradun's Welham Prep and later at the Doon School. A chip off the old block, he was an ace sportsman like his grandfather. He was awarded the house colours in Class IX and his games blazer the following year. These were incredible achievements, for such honours are rarely conferred upon students at such an early stage. He received the school colours for squash, boxing and swimming and was declared the best PT leader of the year. Where his grandfather had once ruled Mayo's wrestling arena, Kheenvsar's young prince was winning bout after bout in the Doon School's boxing ring. He rose to become the heavyweight champion and was the sole student of his batch to have won the gold medal. Raja Gajendra Singhji graduated from The Doon School after captaining Jaipur House and, like his grandfather, passed his final examinations with a first division.

King of the Court

Raja Gajendra Singhji moved from hostel life in Dehradun to hostel life at Delhi University's North Campus as an undergraduate of the famed St. Stephen's College. His college contemporaries still remember the squash ball echoing upon being powerfully struck with his racquet. The erstwhile star heavyweight became the king of St

Stephen's court, and news of his mastery over squash spread far and wide. In 1977, he won his first national level championship at his home court against Ananth Nayak. Cupid had struck Delhi's damsels as Kheenvsar's scion rode his motorbike in a fashionable pair of bell-bottoms, true to the style of the 1970s.

Raja Gajendra Singhji made his way into the Indian squash team. Unfortunately, he contracted malaria prior to their tour to Pakistan. After recovering, India's national squash champion was waving the nation's flag overseas. Thanks to his squash scholarship, Raja Gajendra Singhji earned the opportunity to pursue his second undergraduate degree at Canada's University of Western Ontario. Here, he met the famed coach, Jack Fairs, who continued to churn out squash champions well past his 90th birthday. From this point onwards, there was no looking back for the squash maestro. The list of his squash achievements is endless, but a few major milestones that he recounts are as follows:

National Squash Achievements

Year	*Tournament*	*Position*
1977	All-India Junior National Squash Championship	Winner
1978	World Cup Championship	Member of Indian Team
	Central India Men's Open Championship	Winner
	Rajasthan Open	Winner

Year	Tournament	Position
	Northern India Open	Runner-Up
	Maharashtra Junior State Championship	Winner
	Delhi Junior State Championship	Winner
	Central India Junior Championship	Winner
	Inter Collegiate Championship, Delhi	Winner
	All-India University Championship	Winner

International Squash Achievements

Tournament	Position
World Ranking by the Professional Squash Association (PSA)	33
US Open (Seattle)	Semi-finalist
Canadian Open	Semi-finalist
Ontario Open	Champion
Canadian Ranking	II
US Intercollegiate Championship	Winning Team

Note: The last listing is significant because the US Intercollegiate Championship is contested between various colleges from the Unites States, Canada and Mexico. The University of Western Ontario was the first Canadian team to win the title.

Other positions he held are as follows:

Captain of St. Stephen's College & Delhi University squash teams

Squash colours at St. Stephen's College, Delhi University

Two to Tango

Ahead of his final year at the University of Western Ontario, Raja Gajendra Singhji made a homeward trip to visit his family. Over a cup of tea, his parents introduced him to the lady who would soon become his life partner. A young princess from Gamph, Priti Kumari Chudasama enchanted the Canadian-return with her simplicity and naïve charm.

Early Years

Rani Priti Kumari was born on 4 January 1961, to Kunwar Dilawar Singhji of Gamph and his wife, Kunwarani Rajendra Kumari, from Sarila. She spent her childhood in the southern tea estates, where her father worked as a tea manager for James Finlay & Co. While growing up in the blissful, undulating estates of Kannan Devan, Rani Priti Kumari studied at Ooty's prestigious Nazareth Convent. Thereafter, she pursued her diploma at Bangalore's Jyoti Nivas College.

A talented rollerblader, horse rider and markswoman, she discovered her penchant for patisserie and baking. To gain world-class training from the best, she departed for a bakery course in Bern, Switzerland, where her maternal uncle resided. During her training days, her parents received her marriage proposal from Kheenvsar.

Her maternal aunts, who resided in Jaipur, arranged a meeting between her and the scion of Kheenvsar in November 1981. Raja Gajendra Singhji was instantly smitten by her, and within three months, on 25 February 1982, the two were married in a stylish wedding ceremony at Jaipur's Civil Lines.

Canada Days

Soon after, they returned to Canada, where Raja Gajendra Singhji was to complete his final semester. They resided in the married students' accommodation near campus. From the pleasantly temperate climate of Munnar, Rani Priti Kumari now found herself contending with a typical Canadian winter, with temperatures plummeting to –40 degrees Celsius. She remembers spending a relatively lonely couple of months in Canada while her husband attended his varsity squash tours. Rani Priti Kumari even recalls having to make proxy attendances on his behalf in class, sitting beside his campus friends to hurriedly jot down notes that he would study before his exams.

Accustomed to her solitary life in the tea gardens, Rani Priti Kumari adjusted to Canada fairly well. Her affable nature gained her many friends on campus, and she took to cross-country skiing in her free time. Raja Gajendra Singhji's cousin sister and her husband resided in Deep River, Ontario, which was at a fair distance. The newlyweds visited them every now and then.

If one is to imagine Raja Gajendra Singhji's days of squash eminence in Canada, a rosy picture comes to mind. In reality, he struggled to fulfil his sporting dreams. When he obtained a scholarship to the University of Western Ontario, Raja Gajendra Singhji faced much reluctance from his father. His mother sponsored his plane ticket to Canada.

As an overseas student, Raja Gajendra Singhji lived a hand-to-mouth existence. His scholarship and squash tutoring income aside, he had to rely on odd jobs to supplement his rent money when it fell short. He remembers planting trees in the dense Canadian forests and mowing lawns in Florida. Oftentimes, he took up babysitting, but his absolute revulsion towards infant faeces caused him to be fired. Raja Gajendra Singhji narrates the incident of when he made the baby's older sibling change the diapers. Just then, the parents walked in and caught him red-handed. Needless to say, he was promptly turned out.

Because his student visa prevented him from performing extensive work overseas, he was compelled to borrow his generous friend's name to work in a toy factory. Raja Gajendra Singhji stitched together stuffed Frankensteins as an unsuspecting Bob Rooney. A proud father of six children, the real Bob Rooney is today a thriving businessman in Alberta and remains a close friend of Raja Gajendra Singhji.

Twin Bereavements

Life was passing by fairly peacefully in Ontario until the following year, which heralded devastating news. A road accident near Coimbatore in September 1983 had claimed Rani Priti Kumari's father's life. She hurried back to India to mourn her father and lend a shoulder to her newly widowed mother, Majisab Rajendra Kumari. Rani Priti Kumari had a younger brother, Jaideep, who looked after their mother so she could resume her duties as a new bride and daughter-in-law. In less than two years, fate would strike yet again. Jaideep Sinhji, too, met with a motorcycle accident in Bangalore in June 1985. A van that swerved onto the wrong side of the road collided head-on with his bike, and Jaideep Sinhji succumbed to a brain haemorrhage.

Before the accident, he was about to commence his job in the same tea estates where his father had served. He was also planning on marrying Sangeeta Sen, the love of his life whom he met during his college days in Bangalore. All of this was snatched away in the blink of an eye, and Majisab Rajendra Kumari was left dumbfounded with grief. Her daughter was all that she had left in this world, and Raja Gajendra Singhji made no delay in coming to the rescue of his bereaved mother-in-law.

Majisab Rajendra Kumariji of Gamph

On her wedding day

Any ode written to the house of Kheenvsar remains unfinished without a special mention to Majisab Rajendra Kumariji of Gamph.

After suffering the twin bereavements in her family,

Majisab Rajendra Kumariji relocated to Jaipur with her son-in-law's help. Contrary to her earlier plans of settling down alongside her tea estate friends in Coorg, Majisab Rajendra Kumari agreed to settle down close to her daughter. Her two sisters, Saral Kumari and Sneh Kumari, also resided in Jaipur because their husbands, Kunwar Shivraj Singh and Colonel Thakur Govind Singhji, both hailed from the Khatipura family.

Gamph's Majisab moved into a bungalow in a colony neighbouring Civil Lines in Jaipur and then eventually moved in with her daughter's family. She spent the rest of her life between Kheenvsar Fort in the village and Jaipur's Kheenvsar House. Majisab Rajendra Kumari enjoyed spending time at the family's two Himalayan abodes as well. Her son-in-law often expressed his fascination at her ability to live a solitary life in the already-isolated estate of Gushaini in Tirthan for months on end.

She formed an integral part of the Kheenvsar household, seasoning it with her heavy Bundelkhandi accent. Drop-dead gorgeous as she had been in her heydays, Majisab Rajendra Kumari aged so gracefully that she turned heads even in her last decade. Independent, outspoken and free-spirited, her Bundela heritage governed her unique persona. Every so often, she vividly recalled stories from her younger days in Sarila and her time at the tea estates in the south.[1]

She made sure to keep in frequent touch with all her near and dear ones and maintained a telephone book with everyone's numbers. She journalled sporadically and is remembered for her beautiful handwriting. Majisab Rajendra Kumari bore an unknown culinary gift. She effortlessly churned out self-invented delicacies from her kitchen that left her many nieces, nephews and grandchildren coming back for more. The television remained her constant companion, and she particularly liked drama serials and talent shows.

She was such a stickler for cleanliness that only the most obdurate household help could serve her. A heavy smoker, she used to ash her cigarette in various corners of the house to test the staff persons' attentiveness while cleaning.

Even though destiny had been cruel to her, Majisab Rajendra Kumari kept a mile's distance from self-pity. She was resilient and vivacious even in solitary times. She lived to the age of 88 and saw all three of her great-grandchildren before ascending to the heavens in January 2024.

The Return to India

Their Canadian chapter ended with the freshly graduated prince returning to his rural homeland with his consort in 1984. They initially took to farming on their ancestral lands and raised agricultural revenue. Back then, Kheenvsar Fort was a humble dwelling, and Rani Priti Kumari reminisces about the days when they itinerantly lodged in the fort's various guest rooms. The duo remembers their humbler days of commuting in a second-hand Bajaj Tempo Matador and saving bit by bit to fortify their present-day empire.

Their firstborn arrived on 4 May 1986. The future inheritor of the Karamsot legacy was named Dhananjai. Bearing the most striking set of eyes, he was so beautiful that he qualified as a poster baby in every sense of the word. As his chapter will come to elaborate, as a child, Dhananjai was the equivalent of Dennis the Menace, and his various mischiefs took everyone by storm.

Six years later, in the very same maternity chamber of Jaipur's Santokba Durlabhji Memorial Hospital, they brought me into this world. It was a rainy morning on 6 July 1992, when at 7.55 a.m., the hospital's nurses announced, 'It's a girl!' My mother beamed with joy because she had wished to have a girl child this time. Neha, Priya, Nandini, there was a list of names awaiting me, but my brother intervened and insisted on calling me by no other name than Urvashi. Urvashi Ma'am happened to be his favourite school teacher, whom he admired so much as to name his younger sister after her. Back then, most of northern India was hesitant to name its daughters after mythological *apsaras* or celestial nymphs, but not my family. We will return to my brother and I in the forthcoming chapters.

Hoteliering Glory

The year 1992 wasn't just special for being the year I was born. It was also the year my grandfather, Raja Onkar Singhji, handed over Kheenvsar Fort's governance to my father. What had been a young heritage hotel of the 80s entered its most transformative stage. Under my father, Khimsar Fort entered its golden age, with multiple stages of development. Trees were planted all around Kheenvsar by means of drip irrigation, and from an arid settlement, the fort flourished into a verdant tourist attraction.

The fort's older wings were refurbished, and newer

complexes were added. In 1999, Kheenvsar Fort received the Best Grand Heritage Hotel of India from the then Prime Minister Shri Atal Bihari Vajpayee and has remained among India's leading heritage hotels ever since.

In the early 2000s, Raja Gajendra Singhji created a second hotel in the Khimsar Group of Hotels. It was a spectacular dunes resort located 6 kilometres from the fort, with luxury huts, a bar, a restaurant and a heavenly oasis in between.

Today, Khimsar Fort holds the keys to 89 luxuriously designed rooms and conference and banquet facilities; Khimsar Dunes Village is home to 18 luxurious huts around a spectacular oasis. Both properties are affiliated with the ITC Group of Hotels and are highly sought-after destinations by travellers from all around the world. They have attracted a plethora of film shootings, destination weddings and high-end corporate events.

Rajasthan's long and simmering summer months necessitate an enduring off-season for its hotels. Every year, during these months, Raja Gajendra Singhji and Rani Priti Kumari made their way to the Himalayas. Around the start of the millennium, they built a 5-acre estate in the Tirthan Valley of Himachal Pradesh to serve as their summer retreat. Then, in 2015, the Khimsar Group of Hotels inaugurated its third property, named after me as Urvashi's Retreat, in the heavenly outskirts of Manali.

Raja Gajendra Singhji's genius isn't limited to the hotel business. He undertook the daring and Herculean task of creating Kheenvsar's present-day family residence, Dhananjai Vilas. He is too humble to admit that this monumental building is among the most glorious private estates of its times. Apart from Kheenvsar and Manali, other cities within his key correspondence network, such as Jaipur, Jodhpur and New Delhi, were swept into this enterprise of meteoric expansion. The rate of development in the neighbouring villages too rose in congruence with his political stronghold in Rajasthan.

The People's King

Raja Gajendra Singhji marked his electoral debut in Rajasthan's state legislative assembly elections in 1998 as an independent candidate from Nagaur. His tremendous performance as an independent candidate was noteworthy and resulted in him being granted a ticket by BJP's Vasundhara Raje Scindia in the subsequent state elections.

As BJP's candidate from Nagaur, Raja Gajendra Singhji emerged with a landslide victory and was sworn in as the Minister of Energy in Raje's Government that presided over Rajasthan from 2003 to 2008. Thereafter, with delimitation being imposed on his erstwhile constituency, he was assigned candidacy from Lohawat, which elected him for his second consecutive term. This time, Raje's government formed the opposition to Gehlot's Indian National Congress. Raja Gajendra Singhji committed a political hat-trick in 2013 when the people of Lohawat re-elected him as their representative and he rightfully earned a way into Raje's cabinet. By now, he had become a veteran and expressed no reluctance when Raje handed him multiple portfolios of gigantic stature, namely Industries, Energy, Sports, the Delhi

Mumbai Industrial Corridor (DMIC) and Environment.

Since his victory in the 2023 state elections, he has been serving Rajasthan as its health minister and is the senior-most member in Shri Bhajanlal Sharmaji's government.

His sequential electoral victories point towards his success as an elected representative. Rajasthan's myriad political, diplomatic and administrative offices continue to remember Raja Gajendra Singhji's numerous tenures for his transparency, efficiency and honesty. His voters join his long list of admirers for his non-partisan and forthright ways. Apart from making crucial infrastructural breakthroughs in Lohawat and the various administrative domains under his charge, Raja Gajendra Singhji brought about an era of renewed development.

He generously donated parts of his ancestral land for various purposes of social welfare. Kheenvsar's bus stand, its sports stadium and a Rajput boys' hostel have materialized due to his charitable efforts. His recent ventures into real estate have brought Kheenvsar two marketplaces and a thriving set of colonies for residential and commercial purposes.

Raja Gajendra Singhji's cumulative efforts have positioned Kheenvsar as an important commercial hub of its region. The people of Kheenvsar recently welcomed its first district-level hospital. While driving into Kheenvsar, one crosses the Karamsi Circle, a roundabout with a magnificent statue of the Karamsot founder at its centre. Opposite the fort's entrance stands another horse-mounted statue of his beloved grandfather, Thakur Kesri Singhji.

Thakur Kesri Singhji's statue in Khimsar

By now, it is easy to fathom that the individual legacy of Raja Gajendra Singhji requires a separate book. Soon to be 68, the exemplary torchbearer of the Karamsots remains unparalleled in every way. It is no wonder that he is often equated with Emperor Akbar for his unprecedented achievements in every sphere of his life.

His extensive list of professional achievements notwithstanding, Raja Gajendra Singhji is a thorough family man, a loyal friend and an upright, virtuous and foresighted man of his times. Throughout his evolution, Rani Priti Kumari played a cardinal role as the ideal life partner, friend, confidant, mother, daughter-in-law, mother-in-law and grandmother.

Kunwar Dilawar Singhji of Gamph with Kunwarani Rajendra Kumari on their wedding day

Similar to her father, the late Kunwar Dilawar Singhji, Kheenvsar's Ranisab was loved and adored by all. Compassionate, beautiful and charming, her childish simplicity thrived alongside her supreme wisdom.

Rani Priti Kumari was a deeply spiritual and emotionally intelligent woman. She carried a deep interest in the fields of psychology and psychosomatic wellness. She overcame her arachnophobia after visiting Dr Warren Stag, a famed kinesiologist in Pune. After this particular episode of healing, Rani Priti Kumari placed deep faith in this stream of wellness. She followed the path of Vipassana for many years and continued to practice the yogic and meditative teachings of Sadhguru via the Isha foundation.

Rani Priti Kumari was also an avid cinephile and lover of music. Psychological genres of cinema appealed to her, as did the complete written works of Sydney Sheldon. She particularly admired the cinematic legacy of Amitabh Bachchan and had a diverse palette for Indian and international pop music and even opera. Until Spotify and Apple Music took over, it was impossible to spot Rani Priti Kumari without her beloved radio that she'd listen to for hours on end.

Until her last days, Rani Priti Kumari cheerfully planted flowers in both her estates in Himachal Pradesh. She took immense pride in being a planter's daughter and left the gardens in full bloom.

As a family person, she had been the centring force in the Kheenvsar household. Rani Priti Kumari was the steadfast pillar for her family. In a cruel twist of fate, she departed for her heavenly abode in the early hours of 5 June 2025. All of 64 years of age, she is believed to have suffered from a silent heart attack that left everyone in utter shock and disbelief. It would be remiss of me, not only as her daughter but also as the author of this saga, to fall short of expressing my deepest appreciation for her selfless role in shaping us into who we are today.

Baisaraj Sunita Kumariji

The Humble Princess

Thakur Onkar Singhji and Thakurani Sneh Lata gave birth to a baby girl on 2 June 1964, whom they named

Sunita, meaning the daughter of Dharma. Baisa Sunita Kumariji pursued her early education at Welham Girls' School, Dehradun, and completed her undergraduate at Jaipur's Kanoria College.

Soon after, in 1985, she was introduced to Kunwar Shardul Narayan Singhji, a young Baghel noble from Tirwa in Uttar Pradesh. He happened to be Raja Gajendra Singhji's junior by a few years at the Doon School. A newly married Kunwarani Sunita Kumariji carried her beloved desert homeland within her heart to Lucknow, the City of Nawabs, where she has lived ever since.

Baisa Sunita Kumariji has exhibited talent in several spheres, such as the culinary and fine arts, and is a devout follower of bhakti. She and Kunwar Shardul Narayan Singhji were blessed with their firstborn, Bhanej Baisa Bhavini Singh, on 2 February 1988, and then a son, Bhanej Bana Trivikram Singh, on 3 April 1993.

Bhavini Baisa is a professional graphic designer and graduate of Baroda's prestigious Maharaja Sayajirao University. In December 2020, she married Kunwar Anirudh Singhji Jadon, a Rajput from Nagaliya, Uttar Pradesh. His father, Lieutenant General Ashok Singhji (retd), is an ex-army officer who served as the Commanding-in-Chief of the Southern Command. Kunwar Anirudh Singhji is an eminent orthodontist and is currently practicing in Navi Mumbai. Bhavini Baisa is a graphic designer by profession and is currently juggling her work with motherhood. She and Kunwar Anirudh Singhji were blessed with their daughter, Aranyani, in 2021.

Baisa Sunita Kumari, along with her relative, Kunwarani Pratibha Kumari, and daughter, Bhavini

Baisa, jointly manage their venture, Suprabha. A highly sought-after saree brand, Suprabha is their labour of love that works with Lucknow's artisans to produce sarees in varied craft styles. *Badla, mukaish, zardozi,* thread embroidery and shadow work are some of the styles that Suprabha is known for.

Baisa Sunita Kumariji's son, Trivikram Singh, is a Doon School alumnus like his father. After working in the sales sector of ITC's hotel division, he returned to Lucknow to attend to his family businesses. In February 2025, he married Tripti Kumari, who hails from Daspan, Rajasthan.

Baisa Sunita Kumari spends most of her time immersed in bhakti under the tutelage of Swami Kaushik Chaitanya Maharaj. She is a diligent reader of the Sundar Kaand and is a devout follower of Lord Rama.

20

Kunwar Dhananjai Singh and Kunwarani Mrigesha Kumari

Kheenvsar's Millennial Dawn

When Raja Gajendra Singhji and Rani Priti Kumari gazed at their newborn, the first feature they noticed was his strikingly beautiful pair of eyes. They were large, almond-shaped and echoing with laughter. Rani Priti Kumari named her little bundle of mischief Dhananjai, the embodiment of fire, inheritor of wealth and a modern-day reincarnation of the Pandava, Arjuna.

Growing up, there wasn't a single dull moment around Kunwar Dhananjai Singhji. Whether in the backseat of a car during long journeys or at play on lazy afternoons, he was usually giggling and skirling about with his companions. Marwari was the first language he picked up, and trust Kheenvsar's Dennis the Menace to replace his playschool's 'good morning' with a '*khamaghani*', a salutation that he taught many of his classmates at Loharu Montessori School. The monochromatic world of academics spelt boredom in his dictionary, and Kunwar Dhananjai Singhji would rather be out catching butterflies and playing cricket.

He followed in his father's footsteps to become a squash champion at Ajmer's Mayo College. He is among the rare Dosco sons who was enrolled in the rival Mayo College. The credit for this decision belongs solely to Rani Priti Kumari, who preferred sending Kunwar Dhananjai Singhji to a school that was closer to home and to Rajput-centric values and tradition.

Kheenvsar's 21st-century scion carved his own legacy as a prolific debater, dramatist, photographer and one of the most happy-go-lucky boys of his batch. He received critical acclaim for playing the role of Dr Kraus at an annual inter-house play competition. Further, his brilliant rebuttals on the debate podium won him numerous accolades. He went to Mayo's Colvin House and captained its squash team in his final year.

He then went on to pursue a degree in hospitality overseas. After a brief hospitality course in Melbourne, Kunwar Dhananjai Singhji proceeded to study at the world's leading Glion Institute in Switzerland. However, much as Kunwar Dhananjai Singhji carried the inherited familial legacy of hoteliers, his true passions lay in the sphere of politics and vintage automobiles.

Admiring Atal Bihari Vajpayee as his role model, his extempore speeches left audiences rapt. Kunwar Dhananjai Singhji played a crucial role in all of his father's electoral campaigns and swept the youth vote banks in his favour. At present, his popularity among the youth of Rajasthan makes him one of the state's most followed youth icons on social media and a chief contender to preside over the Rajasthan Cricket Association.

The bright and competent youth leader has many heights to achieve when it comes to the governance of his state and nation.

Young legacy holders such as Kunwar Dhananjai Singhji truly empathize with the poor and disadvantaged strata of society. To give back to his community, Kunwar Dhananjai Singhji founded the Annadata Charitable Trust, a far-reaching NGO that addresses numerous socio-economic issues through more than 12 impactful projects. Annadata Charitable Trust's outreach in Western Rajasthan has barely left any stone unturned. From education, COVID-19 relief and funding for the poor and underprivileged, it has spread into arenas of environmental awareness, water conservation and assistance for the specially abled. In touching thousands of lives, Kunwar Dhananjai Singhji aspires to impact many, many more.

His key business venture emerged out of the foundation of Tirupati Mines, a mining enterprise close to Kheenvsar. He has also taken up a brave new venture by the name of Khimsar Minecorp, which could be the ultimate game changer in Kunwar Dhananjai Singhji's entrepreneurial career. He has the foresight to dream and the determination to achieve.

His multifarious persona as a next-gen Karamsot custodian notwithstanding, the *avatar* worth marvelling over is Kunwar Dhananjai Singhji, the petrolhead. What began as a mere hobby for cars was soon overtaken by a voracious appetite for vintage automobile restoration. Year after year, and car after car, Dhananjai rapidly ascended among India's vintage automobile fraternity as one of its foremost collectors. His vast fleet of cars and motorcycles, all vintage, are housed at the Khimsar automobile garage, astonishing every visitor and passer-by.

Glistening bonnets, retro tail lights, finely polished metallic grills and an exceptional collection of vintage cars are where Dhananjai's heart truly lies. However, this does not imply his apathy for state-of-the-art machines; Kunwar Dhananjai Singhji has them all too. From India's only Moto Guzzi to the Ducatis, Indian Chiefs, Triumphs and BMWs that few can only dream of, Kunwar Dhananjai Singhji's personal garage has them all. He isn't shy to vroom past in his red Porsche on a crisp highway or ramble along a dirt track in his scarlet-coloured Thar. The list, coupled with his collection of miniature models and antiques, makes for the most extensive collection to have been curated in the history of the Karamsots. It can be said without doubt that Kunwar Dhananjai Singhji equates Russia's Catherine the Great in daringly installing what I imagine would be perceived in hindsight as another Hermitage in the making.

Many sport the slogan of 'Carpe Diem' on their social media handles and smartphone covers, but when it comes to really living it large, Kunwar Dhananjai Singhji is as authentic as one gets. His gloriously enriched life only became more eventful in 2012 when he met his better half. Rajkot's eldest princess, Mrigesha Kumari Jadeja, entered his neatly ordered life like a gust of fresh air and changed it forever. Where Kunwar Dhananjai Singhji is organized and steadfast, Kunwarani Mrigesha's easy-going and adventurous spirit provides the perfect counterbalance. She added her ringing laughter and native charm to his erstwhile wine, cheese and jazz-saturated confines. Her rich upbringing as per Vedic values and a thorough understanding of ancient Indian wisdom reached every corner of the Kheenvsar household with a levelheadedness uncharacteristic of our depleted times.

Born to Rajkot's Raja Mandhata Sinhji and Rani Kadambari Deviji Jadeja, Kunwarani Mrigesha Kumari is the oldest of their three children and the darling of Ranjit Vilas Palace. An ace athlete and badminton player, Kunwarani Mrigesha pursued her education at Jain International School in Bangalore and then moved to Mumbai's Narsee Monjee College for her Senior Cambridge. She graduated from Mithibai College and is a qualified teacher in elementary education. Kheenvsar's young and vivacious Kunwarani Sahiba upholds vegan ethics in her nutritional consumption and is an ardent supporter of animal rights organizations such as PETA.

She also has a flair for fine arts and jewellery design and

has recently begun showcasing some of her handiworks through her home studio, Rang. Her customized nose pins have risen in demand, but Mrigesha chooses to craft these at an unhurried, anti-commercialized pace. Her other works include acrylic art on sarees, inspired by her highly creative and enterprising mother.

Over the course of their decade-long alliance, Kunwar Dhananjai Singhji and Kunwarani Mrigesha have raised three beautiful children, Mrignaini, Shivagami and Sangram. The diva Mrignaini, athletic Shivagami and mischievous Sangram form an endearing trio. As a wise person once said, 'The apple doesn't fall far from the tree,' and the three little ones testify the truthfulness of this saying.

It is for them, as Kheenvsar's youngest generation, that I leave behind this living archival saga. May they inherit and aptly nourish it with their own narratives and accounts. My greatest gift to them as their aunt is the benefit of recorded hindsight over a glorious ancestry that spans over 20 generations. May they find the innate capability of appreciating the courage with which their forefathers and foremothers followed their dharma, and may it help them derive the purpose in following their own.

Before drafting my epilogue, I deliberately leave the forthcoming chapter open for them to fill in the time to come. I have kept this book open-ended with the simple intention of reminding Mrignaini, Shivagami, Sangram and my readers of its enduring, living spirit. History derives many of its beauties and limitations from never being set in stone. We are limited in what we know but surrender eternally by accepting the unknown. The narratives we have access to are known only because they happened to survive while countless counter-narratives perished. Because they perished, the forgotten and unknown narratives must be accorded our respect for the mysterious possibilities that are submerged. These possibilities could have changed the course of history and reality in unthinkable, unimaginable ways. For all we know, there could come a moment when they are unearthed, revealed and known, thus changing the course of history once again but never forever because history has ethereal ways of panning out. Sometimes, it gives away; other times, it chooses to withhold. As tiny microcosms floating amidst history's various dress rehearsals, we are, at best, left with its evasive residue.

21

Baisaraj Mrignaini, Baisaraj Shivagami and Bhanwar Sangram Singh

The Next Generation of Karamsot Rathores

Mrignaini Kumari

A Charming Diva

Born in the Pink City on 14 May 2015, Mrignaini is the first of Dhananjai and Mrigesha's three children. Currently a student at the Maharani Gayatri Devi School, Jaipur, Mrignaini is full of beans and spreads joy wherever she goes. Her dancing talent is at its zenith when she performs the *ghoomar* in her traditional finery.

A doting older sister, Mrignaini is an animal lover and enjoys wildlife photography with her paternal grandfather. Her razor-sharp wit often has us all in splits. Off late, she's become an ardent listener of Lana Del Rey.

Shivagami Kumari

A Budding Athlete

Three-and-a-half years later, on 14 December 2018, the family was blessed with another baby girl, Shivagami.

Mrignaini instantly found her friend, companion and partner in crime in Shivagami. A born athlete, Shivagami runs faster than the wind. She's a promising squash player and has a genuine knack for any and every sport she has tried her hand at. Her brilliance extends to the classroom as well, where she's an ace scholar. When it comes to dancing, she looks up to her sister, but her choice of music tilts more towards Shakira.

Shivagami is a fangirl of Shahid Kapoor and Kriti Sanon and had an endearing phase when she believed she was SIFRA, the robot.

Sangram Singh

The Dynamite

The youngest of the three, Sangram was born prematurely on 13 November 2019. He grew up to be a confident, dashing and highly affectionate young man with a deep fascination for swords. A highly intelligent and imaginative child, Sangram can mesmerize everyone with his storytelling skills. His inventive thoughts and observational comedy make him a people's magnet, and he carries adulation for Shantipriya from *Om Shanti Om*.

Epilogue

It isn't by coincidence that I've excluded my section in this book. Just as a photographer makes for an awkward subject, writers such as myself find the act of writing about themselves strange and painstaking. However, I find it worthwhile to recount my serendipitous encounter with this glorious body of work.

As a postgraduate student at LSE, I dedicated my master's thesis to my various ancestresses of Kheenvsar whose fates were incinerated by the virtue of committing sati. Much as I admire their courage and virtue, I am equally overwhelmed by their unflinching sacrifices that ascertained our survival. It is owing to these bravehearts that their progeny has thrived and is now empowered to tell its own story.

Back then, I did not imagine that in the short span of six years, I would be bestowed with the responsibility of translating this gargantuan historical saga of the Karamsot Rathores. Transforming the scholarly works that Dr Mahendra Singhji Tanwar painstakingly compiled over eight long years has been no small feat. On the contrary, the telling or retelling of somebody else's story is an endeavour that cannot repeat itself in the same manner. Just as every occurrence of history carries its set of rarities, so does its retelling. Similar to the ever-flowing course of history, its narrations know no bounds. History might momentarily dwell upon interludes, but its richness predates and outlives the mortal soul so as to humble us through each retelling.

Many turn to historical sources to validate their identity and ego, often overlooking history's true essence: the humility of witnessing time's ceaseless unfolding through events and coincidences as unpredictable as their chronicling. This historical narrative didn't perish beneath others; it survived to be retold and known in a version that might be starkly different from its objective occurrences. Thus, by abstaining from limiting history to one known version, we expand to embrace its multifarious essence. For the scholar and the historian, the acknowledgement of the unknown is equally, if not more, important than what is presently known. Limitless possibilities exist in accepting that one can never entirely fathom the randomized progression of time. The blending of historical form with fiction doesn't seem as absurd then, for oftentimes, historical inferences rely on sources that are as fragile and porous as human memory. All in all, we jointly take pride in and celebrate the versions of history that survive until our time and must treat them responsibly for their continued survival with minimal tarnishes of the human ego.

As the translator of this version, I have constantly tried to desist from overindulging in the romanticized realms of historical mystery; even then, I am far from attaining perfection. Among the various ironies of history, one that is poignantly phrased by John F. Kennedy reads, 'History is a relentless master. It has no present, only the past rushing into the future. To try to hold fast is to be swept aside.' In our occupation of the present, we are the custodians of many stories that predate us. Just as ours might outlive us in our brief journey through this mortal realm. Hence, I have derived an immense sense of responsibility from treating history in the same way I hope our fleeting present will be regarded in the future.

Another irony resides in the fact that after all these centuries of Karamsot history, destiny chanced upon one of its daughters as its humble chronicler. From a time when women's participation in historical narratives was negligible to the present day when a daughter of the dynasty reclaims those very narratives, if this isn't historical vindication, then what is?

Countless weavers of history have walked the Earth. A select few have followed their destiny or higher purpose, not for the sake of being remembered but by the virtue of their conscience. As their inheritors, I hope for each one of us to continue this pursuit. Rao Jodha's moral discretion pierced through Kumbhalgarh's impregnable gates to avenge his father's deceitful murder. An 86-year-old Rao Karamsiji went down fighting for his clan in the distant grounds of Narnaul. His son, Rao Pichyaansiji, speedily galloped into the battlegrounds of Giri-Sumel despite knowing that he might not return. Similarly, Thakur Zorawar Singhji's loyal virtues kept him away from his motherland in the name of service. The absolute prevalence of moral virtue and dharma can be inferred from every chapter of Karamsot history. Even more marvellous is the fact that these stories form a microcosm of the larger Karamsot and Rathore legacy, which history continues to assimilate through various mediums and expressions.

Even though the mediums and formats of service have changed, our world today demands moral sincerity at unprecedented scales. Dharma or our sense of moral duty must be performed as an end rather than a superficial means to historical recognition. Through and through, an absolute desistance from our ego unites and summarizes these imperatives.

Lastly, I hope that this modest contribution on my part adds to the ever-expanding realm of narrative representation. Much of our strength as a human race lies in our diversity, for it encourages us to learn from others' lessons. No matter how disjointed two narratives may appear in terms of chronology or geography, they remain inextricably connected, for both emerge from the human condition. Human experience, after all, is enriched by means of its relatability and timeless relevance. May it further humanity's evolutionary thirst for knowledge, and may it consolidate our acceptance of the unknown. These intermingling stories somewhat establish that far away, amidst the Thar desert of erstwhile Rajputana, there lay an ancestry that was as fierce, brave, loyal and virtuous as they come. And come they do, time and again, for the world's history is shaped similar to the world itself. It is circular, cyclical and unyielding in its resilience.

Veer Bhogya Vasundhara!

Appendix

The Rathore Family Tree

Acknowledgements

First and foremost, I would like to acknowledge *Data*, my father, Raja Gajendra Singhji, for entrusting me with the monumental task of bringing this book to life. Had it not been for your unwavering belief in my capabilities as a writer, I might never have ventured into the world of historical non-fiction.

My late mother, Rani Priti Kumariji, for having been a patient proofreader and my foremost cheerleader until her last day.

My brother, Dhananjai Singh, and sister-in-law, Mrigesha Kumari, for believing in my authorial prowess.

Mahendra Singhji Tanwar, the man behind Data's vision, and the author of the parent book, *Karamsot Rathoron ka Gauravmayi Itihaas.* Much of this book is based on his research, painstakingly conducted over eight years. I salute your hard work and dedication. I am also deeply grateful for your unending patience, support and guidance throughout my authorial journey. This book is as much yours as it is mine, if not more.

H.H. Maharaja Gaj Singhji II, the living exemplar of the Rathore legacy—thank you for your generous support and words of praise. You are every Rathore's pride and, to me, the most distinguished Maharaja of our times. It is my honour to have you at the launch of my humble book.

My talented sister, Bhavini Singh, for designing this book's cover. As a Karamsot descendent yourself, your contribution to the aesthetics of this venture is all the more meaningful and special.

My agent, Suhail Mathur—thank you for connecting me with my publishers. Your guidance and expertise made this debut possible. I am most appreciative for your faith in my work.

The Rupa team: Shatarupa Dhar, I truly appreciate your accessibility and the prompt handling of the editorial process; Dibakar Ghosh, thank you for your unending patience and support.

Kranti Sen and Dinesh Singh, for sharing photographs timely, whenever I requested them.

And Ankita Dhar, for patiently proofreading my drafts time and again.

Glossary

Amal ka Dastoor	A Persian-Hindustani term meaning 'the practice of administration' or 'the code of governance'. It refers to the customary laws and administrative traditions observed in royal courts, particularly during the Rajput and Mughal eras, defining the conduct and hierarchy within the realm
Avatar	Derived from the Sanskrit word avatāra, meaning 'descent', the term refers to the incarnation or earthly manifestation of a deity, who is believed to assume various forms to restore cosmic balance and righteousness. In broader usage, avatar signifies the embodiment or representation of a divine being, virtue or ideal in human form
Badshah	A Persian-derived title meaning emperor or sovereign ruler. In the Indian subcontinent, the term was historically used to refer to powerful monarchs, most notably the Mughal emperors, who ruled vast territories with supreme authority
Baijilal	A royal title traditionally used in Marwar and other princely states to denote the daughter or consort of a ruling chief or prince, often associated with nobility and high status within the royal household
Bakshi	Treasurer in the royal court

Baradari	A pavilion or building with twelve doors, designed to allow free airflow, often used for gatherings or royal assemblies
Charan	Charans belong to a caste of hereditary genealogists, poets, scholars and storytellers. Historically, they were valued advisors in Rajput courts. By means of their profound poetry, they also preached *kshatriya dharma* to the Rajputs
Charpai	A light bedstead usually made of wooden frames and ropes, upon which the mattress and bedding are placed
Chhatri	An umbrella-shaped cenotaph bearing four pillars built on the cremation ground in honour of Rajputs to commemorate the glorious legacy they left behind
Daavi	Left (direction)
Daroga	Inspector
Deewan	Minister in the royal court
Dharma	A Vedic law of morality, dutifulness, righteousness and virtuosity, loosely translating into one's duty or destined path of life
Durbar	Royal courtroom
Eklingji	An avatar of Lord Shiva, Eklingji is considered the ruling god of Mewar
Falhaari	Food prepared without grains or pulses, typically consumed during Hindu fasts and religious observances
Gaharwar	The Gaharwar or Gahadwala dynasty was a prominent Rajput dynasty that ruled over present-day Uttar Pradesh and Bihar from the 11th to the 13th century. It was established by Chandradeva around 1090 CE

Gangajal	Sacred water from the River Ganga, revered in Hinduism and used in religious rituals, purification and blessings
Ghat	A series of steps leading down to a river or waterbody, often used for bathing, rituals or cremation ceremonies
Ghoomar	A traditional folk dance of Rajasthan, performed by women in graceful circular movements, often during festive and celebratory occasions
Hakim	Physician
Haveli	A traditional mansion or grand townhouse, often built around an open courtyard and adorned with ornate facades, frescoes and carved jharokhas (overhanging windows). Originating from Persian and Mughal architectural influences, havelis became a hallmark of aristocratic and mercantile families across Rajasthan and northern India. Beyond their architectural splendour, they served as living symbols of lineage, prosperity and hospitality—embodying the social and cultural ethos of royal and noble households. In Rajputana, a haveli was not merely a residence, but a reflection of heritage and pride
Howdah	A large, ornate seat or carriage positioned on the back of an elephant, used historically by royalty or nobility during wars, travels, hunting expeditions or ceremonial processions. Often richly decorated with embroidery, silver or gold embellishments, the howdah symbolized prestige, power and grandeur in royal India

Jagir	A Mughal-era word coined for thikanas
Jagirdar	The incumbent chief of a particular jagir
Jauhar	An Indian practice of mass self-immolation by Rajput women to avoid capture, enslavement and rape by an invading army following their defeat
Jeevni	Right (direction)
Jodhawat	Son of Rao Jodhaji
Karkhaan daftari	Executive officer in the royal court
Kayamkhani	The successors of Kayam Singh Chauhan came to be known as Kayamkhanis. These were Rajputs who converted to Islam in the 14th century and were notable for ruling the Fatehpur–Jhunjhunu region in Rajasthan from the 14th to the 18th century
Khejris	Sacred trees (*Prosopis cineraria*) native to Rajasthan, revered for their resilience and significance in local ecology and religious tradition
Khilat	During his time, Aurangzeb deployed the tactic of offering poisoned robes, known as poisoned khilat, to kill his adversaries by betrayal and foul play. Lethal vesicants in the robe's fabric enter the victim's body through their sweat pores, resulting in their death
Khyaat	Documentation done from a historical point of view
Kuldevi	The ancestral female deity of a particular *kul*, clan, lineage or dynasty

Mahirelan	A ceremonial custom observed in Rajput weddings, wherein the bride's family presents gifts, ornaments or tokens of affection to the groom's household. The Mahirelan symbolizes goodwill, familial alliance and the strengthening of kinship ties between the two royal houses
Marudhara	A Sanskrit word combining 'maru', meaning barren, sandy or desert, with 'dhara', meaning earth. Marudhara translates into desert land and lends its nomenclature to the word Marwar
Marwar	A combination of two words, 'maru', meaning barren, sandy or desert, and 'war', meaning fence. Marwar translates into the land protected by the desert. The western region of present-day Rajasthan is known as Marwar for its largely arid landscape
Misal	Precedence in the royal court
Munshi	A clerk, secretary or scribe, often responsible for maintaining records or correspondence, particularly in royal or administrative settings
Nathdwara	An incarnation of Srinathji, a 7-year-old Lord Krishna resides in the temple of Nathdwara, 48 kilometres northeast of Udaipur
Navratri	A nine-night Hindu festival dedicated to the worship of the divine feminine, celebrating the victory of good over evil
Nawab	A title of Persian origin used for a Muslim noble or provincial governor under Mughal rule. It later came to denote semi-autonomous rulers and aristocrats who held authority over regions or estates

Pargana	A group of villages or a district subdivision
Pehelwan	A wrestler or strongman skilled in traditional Indian wrestling, known for strength, discipline and mastery of combat techniques
Pir	A folk-deity venerated for his extraordinary virtues and spirituality
Puja	A ritual act of worship in Hinduism involving offerings, prayers and devotion to deities
Purbiya Rajputs	A term referring to Rajput soldiers from the eastern regions of India, particularly from areas such as Bihar and eastern Uttar Pradesh, who were renowned for their martial skill and often served as mercenaries or soldiers in various royal armies across northern India
Purohit	Purohits are Brahmins by birth and the legitimate conductors of all ceremonies and rituals. They accompanied the king at all times and, when required, even took part in battle
Ranbanka	Ran translates to war. One who met with a heroic end in war came to be hailed as *ranbanka.* A title conferred upon Rathores because each of the first 12 Rathore rulers, from Rao Sihaji to Rao Ranmalji, attained martyrdom on the battlefield
Rao	A title used for the king or *raja*
Rawla	The principal residence or mansion of a noble within a fort's vicinity, typically serving as the private quarters or administrative seat of the Thakur
Safa	A local term for the turban worn across several parts of Rajasthan

Sahib	A term of respect or honour, often used as a suffix with titles or names, such as Thakur Sahib, to denote nobility, authority or esteem
Sardars	Senior Rajput nobles or chieftains appointed by the ruler to advise on matters of governance, justice and military affairs
Sasuraal	A woman's marital home or her husband's family household
Sati	A Hindu sacrificial rite wherein a widow sacrificed her life by sitting atop her deceased husband's funeral pyre
Shastra Puja	A ritual of worship performed to honour weapons, symbolizing respect for valour and the divine power believed to reside in arms; traditionally observed by warriors, especially during Dussehra
Sirayat	Principalities of the first eight jagirdars who were given the *sire ka kurab* during the reign of Sawai Raja Sur Singhji. This status can be equated with the cabinet rank of sacrosanct importance
Sirpech	A jewelled ornament or plume traditionally worn on a turban by Indian royalty and nobility. Often crafted in gold and encrusted with precious stones, the sirpech symbolized rank, honour and regal dignity within the royal court
Subah	A province during the Khalji, Tughlaq and Mughal eras
Subedar	A designated governor of a *subah* or province holding a high rank

Suryavansh	The house of the sun god. Most Rajput clans claim their descent from either the sun god (Suryavanshis), moon god (Chandravanshis) or fire deity (Agnivanshis)
Tavareekh	Daily journal entries
Thaali	A traditional Indian meal served on a round metal platter, comprising a variety of dishes that together offer a balanced representation of regional cuisine. The term also refers to the platter itself on which the meal is arranged
Thakur	The incumbent chief of a particular thikana
Thikana	The smaller unit of a larger kingdom, which a ruler entrusted to his progeny or trusted chieftains. This responsibility included considerable judicial, administrative and stately authority over that particular unit
Yuvraj	A Sanskrit-derived term meaning 'young king' or 'crown prince'. It refers to the heir apparent to a royal throne, traditionally designated to succeed the reigning monarch

Notes

Introduction

1 Mythological origins of the Rajputs distinguish them into three lineages: the Suryavanshis (dynastic descendants of Surya or the Vedic Sun God), Chandravanshis (dynastic descendants of Chandra or the Vedic Moon God) and Agnivanshis (dynastic descendants of Agni or the Vedic God of Fire).

2 Princely states

The Ancestors of Rao Karamsiji

1 Ojha, Gauri Shankar, 'History of the Jodhpur State: Part I', *The History of Rajputana,* Vol. IV, Part I, Vedic Yantralaya, Ajmer, 1938, 57.

2 Badayun (or Budaun) and Kannauj are situated in present-day Uttar Pradesh.

3 Muhnot, Nainsi's records from Jodhpur State records and Sindhayach Dayaldas' records; Nagar, Mahendra Singh, *Rao Jodha Purva Marwar ka Itihaas,* Maharaja Man Singh Pustak Prakash Research Centre, 2019, 1–10.

4 Reu, Pandit Bisheshwar Nath, *Marwar ka Itihaas Part I,* 1938, 4–6.

5 Ibid., 47

6 Ibid., 48

7 Ojha, Gaurishankar Harishchand, *Jodhpur Rajya ka Itihaas Part I,* 1938, 107–108.

8 Reu, Pandit Bisheshwar Nath, *Marwar ka Itihaas Part I*, 1938, 51.

9 Parihars or Pratihars are a prominent Rajput clan, claiming they are descendants of Agni, the Vedic God of Fire. Parihars ruled several parts of Rajasthan from the 6th to the 9th century. They established their capital in Mandavyapura, which is present-day Mandore.

10 Reu, Pandit Vishweshwarnath, *Marwar ka Itihaas Part I*, 1938, 54.

11 Ibid., 49–50

12 Ibid., 49

13 Lodurva was the first capital of the Bhati dynasty of Jaisalmer.

14 Habsi Ambar Champu was a minister of Ahmednagar, whom the Maharaja of Jodhpur warred with in 1621.

15 Reu, Pandit Bisheshwar Nath, *Marwar ka Itihaas Part I*, 1938, 63.

16 Johiyas are a branch of Bikaneri Rajputs known for being granted the custodianship of Johiyawati (present-day Sri Ganganagar).

17 Indas belong to the highest rank of Pratihar Rajputs and were, at one time, the rulers of Mandore.

Chapter 1: Rao Karamsiji

1 According to *Jodhpur Rajya ki Khyaat*, written by Raghuvir Singh and Manohar Singh Ranawat (p. 55), she was the daughter of Jaisalmer's Rawal Devidas Chachawat. *Rani Manga Bhaton ki Bahi* by Dr Mahendra Singh Nagar (p. 11) and *Bhati Vansh ka Gauravmay Itihaas Part II* by Dr Hukam Singh Bhati (p. 385) also confirm this fact.

2 *Marwar ke Sardaron ka Itihas*, Jild (Folio) III, Granthak, 1949, Maharaja Man Singh Pustak Prakash Research Centre, Durg Jodhpur.

3 *Kayam Khan Raasa* was written by a Muslim poet who went by the pseudonym of Kavi Jaan. Kavi Jaan, *Kayam Khan Raasa,* Dr Dasharatha Sharma and Agarchand Nahata (eds.), 36–37, 432–436.

4 Reu, Vishwendranath, *Marwar ka Itihaas Part I,* 1938, 103.

5 Parihar, G.R., *Marwar Maratha Sambandh,* 1977, 16.

6 Dr Mahendra Singh Tanwar provides an account of receiving this information from the late Bhanwar Singhji Tantawas in person.

7 Sarang Khan Gakhar was a tribal chieftain from present-day Pakistan. As a result of his submission to the Mughals, he was rewarded by Babur, who appointed him ruler of the Pothohar Plateau in 1520.

8 *Dayaldaas ki Khyaat,* Jild II, Patra 5; Ojha, Gaurishankar Harishchand, *Jodhpur Rajya ka Itihaas Part I,* 1938, 176; Reu, Pandit Bisheshwar Nath, *Marwar ka Itihaas Part I,* 1938, 114.

9 Rao Beeda's son and Rao Bikaji and Rao Karamsiji's brother who was granted custodianship of Chhapar Dronpur during its previous reclamation by the Rathores.

10 Bhati, Dr Hukam Singh, *Bhati Vansh ka Gauravmaya Itihaas Part II,* Rajasthani Granthagar, 2022, 393.

11 Kavi Jaan, *Kayam Khan Raasa,* Dr Dasharatha Sharma and Agarchand Nahata (eds.), 36–37, 432–436.

12 *Kayam Khan Raasa* by Kavi Jaan was composed to shower praise upon Kayam Khan's dynasty, also known as the Kayamkhani dynasty for being descendants of Kayam Khan. He was a Chauhan Rajput born in the 14th century to the ruler of Doraya, a village in present-day Churu, Rajasthan. He and his brothers converted to Islam around 1352 CE during the time of Feroz Shah Tughlaq. The latter named him Kayam Khan. He served as the Governor of Hisar in

present-day Haryana during the reign of Mahmud Shah Tughlaq and Khizr Khan.

13 Devi Prasad Munshi's collection, *Rathoron ki Vanshaavali*; Ojha, Gaurishankar Harishchand, *Jodhpur Rajya ka Itihaas Part I*, 1938, 57; Rathore, Bhoor Singh, *Rajasthan Mein Rathore Samrajya ka Uday aur Vistaar*, Reu, Pandit Bisheshwar Nath, *Marwar ka Itihaas Part I*, 1938, 103.

14 Reu, Pandit Bisheshwar Nath, *Glories of Marwar and The Glorious Rathors*, Archaeological Department, Jodhpur, 1943, 32.

15 Bankidas's records; As per the replicated records of Shyara Chaukdi's Rani Manga Mehtabji, which were commissioned by the house of Kheenvsar in 1939; As per Dholerao's Raoji Shri Sohan Singhji's records.

Chapter 2: Rao Pichyaansiji

1 Rani Prem Kanwar is mentioned as the daughter of a Bhati Rajput called Shyamdas Bhadawat.

2 Dayaldas's records

3 Tessitori, Dr Luigi Pio, *Bardic and Historical Survey of Rajputana*, Asiatic Society, Calcutta, 1917; Ojha, Gaurishankar Harishchand, *Bikaner Rajya ka Itihaas Part I*, 1939.

4 Mewar's Rana Ratan Singhji's queen, Rani Padmavati, is also known as Rani Padmini in historical records.

5 Ojha, Gaurishankar Harishchand, *Jodhpur Rajya ka Itihaas Part I*, 1938, 193.

6 Reu, Pandit Bisheshwar Nath, *Marwar ka Itihaas Part I*, 1938.

7 Ibid.

8 Tharoor, Shashi, *Inglorious Empire*, Aleph Book Company, New Delhi, 2017.

9 Rajput suffixes such as Singh, Sinh and Singha as well as Rajput clans such as Vaghela/Baghel.

10 Rao Kumpaji was the grandson of Rao Akherajji, Rao Jodha's older brother. He went on to establish the branch of Kumpawat Rathores, whose prime stronghold lay in Aasop.

11 Giri and Sumel are situated 75 kilometres southwest of Ajmer.

12 Muhnot, Nainsi's records from Jodhpur State records; Sindhayach Dayaldas' records, 82.

13 Ibid., 79–80

14 Gehlot, J., *Marwar Rajya ka Itihaas,* Jodhpur State Archives, Maharaja Man Singh Pustak Prakash Research Centre, Jodhpur, 1991, 106.

15 Ibid., 107

16 Ibid.

Chapter 3: Rao Maheshdasji

1 Dewaliya is a village in the Mandalgarh tehsil of Rajasthan's Bhilwara district.

2 A village in Rajasthan's Pali district.

3 A fortress city in Madhya Pradesh's Bundelkhand area.

4 Kheenvsar State Archives, Volume 38, Book 23; Jodhpur State Archives, 86–87.

5 Ibid.

6 Mubarak, Ibn Abul Fazl, *Akbarnama,* 1600–1605, 250; Gehlot, P., *Marwar Rajya ka Itihaas,* Jodhpur State Archives, 109.

7 Mubarak, Ibn Abul Fazl, *Akbarnama,* 1600–1605, 257; Gehlot, P., *Marwar Rajya ka Itihaas,* Jodhpur State Archives, 109.

8 Marwar's erstwhile confederation of sovereign sirayats were undermined as subsidiary jagirs by the royal orders of Jodhpur.

Chapter 4: Thakur Hardasji

1 As per the replicated records of Shyara Chaukdi's Rani Manga Mehtabji commissioned by the house of Kheenvsar on 27 December 1939.

2 Handwritten archive, *Khanp Karamsot*, Maharaja Man Singh Pustak Prakash Research Centre.

3 *Tavareekh Marwaar Ra Thikaana Ri*, Maharaja Man Singh Pustak Prakash Research Centre, 143.

4 Jaitmalji was a Champawat Rathod. Rao Maldeoji's son, Rao Champaji, had a son, Bherudasji. Jaisaji was born to Bherudasji. Jaitmalji was Jaisaji's fifth son, who received Auwa. Later, Auwa was incorporated into the headquarters of the Idanot Champawats.

5 Reu, Pandit Bisheshwar Nath, *Marwar ka Itihaas Part I*, 1938, 248.

6 Shekhawat, Saubhagya Singh, *Rajasthani Veer Geet Part IV*, Rajasthan Oriental Research Institute, Jodhpur, 1979, 72.

7 The Muzaffarid dynasty is also referred to as the Ahmedabad dynasty and is known for serving as the Gujarat Sultanate from 1391 to 1583. The dynasty was founded by Zafar Khan, later known as Muzaffar Shah I, who was the governor of Gujarat during the Tughlaq dynasty of the Delhi Sultanate. In 1398, when Timur wreaked havoc in Delhi, Zafar Khan seized the opportunity and established himself as the sultan of Gujarat. Present-day Ahmedabad was established by his son, Ahmed Shah I. The Muzaffarids continued to rule over Gujarat for the next 200 years before being defeated by the Mughals in 1572; Hasan, Farhat, *State and Locality in Mughal India: Power Relations in Western India, c.1572–1730*, Cambridge University Press, Cambridge, 2004.

8 One of Mota Raja Udai Singh's sons who established the state of Kishangarh.

9 Son and successor of Sawai Raja Sur Singhji; Jodhpur State Records, 150.

10 Ibid., 151

11 Shekhawat, Saubhagya Singh, *Rajasthani Veer Geet Part IV*, Rajasthan Oriental Research Institute, Jodhpur, 1979, 72.

12 Rao Sohan Singhji Dholirao's bards

13 Kalyaan horses belong to a superior pedigree of horses that are either red or black, except for their legs, which are covered in a white coat.

14 Chhota Udaipur or Chhota Udepur is an erstwhile princely state situated in Gujarat's tribal belt adjoining Madhya Pradesh.

Chapter 5: Thakur Dayaldasji

1 As Thakur Dayaldasji was unsuccessful in upholding his word as Maharaja Dalpat Singhji's guarantor, he too was penalized by Shah Jahan.

2 Singhvi is a branch of Oswal Baniyas. People from this family have been appointed to many important posts like *deewan*, *hakam* and *kotwal* in Marwar.

Chapter 6: Thakur Bhim Singhji

1 The Dharmat and Fatehbad combats were fought between Mughal emperor Aurangzeb and Maharaja Jaswant Singhji I of Marwar on 15 April 1658 CE near Ujjain. The latter and Ratlam's Ratan Singhji fought in alliance with Dara Shikoh. Aurangzeb emerged triumphant, and this victory was a crucial milestone in his pursuit to eliminate Dara Shikoh and ascend the Mughal throne. A subsequent confrontation

between Aurangzeb and Dara Shikoh occurred during the Battle of Samugarh on 29 May 1658 CE.

2 Maharaja Jaswant Singhji I served as the chief military officer at Jamrud in Peshawar for the Mughals from 1674 to 1678 CE. He died defending Jamrud from the Afghans during the Sixth Afghan–Mughal War (1667–1668).

Chapter 7: Thakur Harnath Singhji

1 Outraged by Aurangzeb's religious fundamentalism, Mewar, too, joined Marwar's cause until Rana Raj Singhji I's death in 1680 CE, after which Mewar was forced to withdraw support. Aurangzeb had bribed the Rana's men to poison him. His successor, Maharana Jai Singhji, undertook a more diplomatic strategy to broker peace with the Mughals, signing a peace treaty with Aurangzeb in 1681 CE.

Chapter 9: Thakur Zorawar Singhji

1 Built by Muzaffarid King Ahmad Shah I in 1411 CE, Bhadra Fort is located within the walled city of old Ahmedabad.

2 Historians state political motivations behind this assassination because Maharaja Ajit Singhji had gathered much disfavour for his constant refusal to obey the Mughal emperor. Despite Abhay Singhji arriving at Delhi to negotiate peace with the Mughals, they seemed implacable and threatened to annex Marwar. The only condition that they agreed upon to let go of this motive was if the Maharaja (Ajit Singhji) was exterminated.

3 In the Mughal Empire, the Mir Bakshi was the head of the military administration; *Studies in Indian History Volume 4, Rajasthan Through the Ages: Jaipur Rulers and Administration*, R.K. Gupta and S.R. Bakshi (eds.), Sarup & Sons, 2008, 196–197.

4 Jayappaji Scindia was the son of Ranoji Scindia, the founder of Gwalior's Scindia dynasty.

Chapter 10: Thakur Karan Singhji

1 Between present-day Jaitaran and Bar

Chapter 11: Thakur Berisal Singhji

1 'Ot' after a name signifies that the subject(s) in question are the particular person's offsprings. Thus, Zorawarsinghot translates into the son(s) of Thakur Zorawar Singhji. Similarly, Bhomsinghot means the son(s) of Thakur Bhom Singhji. Karamsot is used to collectively refer to all the kindred of Rao Karamsiji.

2 There had been many instances of discord between Jodhpur and Kheenvsar. In the recent past, Jodhpur had taken Kheenvsar and Panchodi from Bhom Singh.

Chapter 12: Thakur Bhopal Singhji

1 Salimkot constitutes a small section of Mehrangarh. Jodhpur was under siege by Sher Shah Suri in 1544 CE. As per historical accounts, he named this section of the fort after his son, Salim, during his visit. Salimkot housed various nobles and dignitaries during their prison sentences.

Chapter 15: Thakur Shardul Singhji

1 Munshi, H.S., Marwar Census Report - 1891.

2 Ibid., 698–699

3 *Indian States: A Biographical, Historical, and Administrative Survey,* Arnold Wright (ed.), Foreign and Colonial Compiling and Publishing Company, 1922, 200.

Chapter 18: Raja Onkar Singhji and Rani Sneh Lata

1 *The Jodhpur Raj Patra*, 22 January 1949, Vol. 84, No. 51, Rajasthan State Archives.

2 Kunwar Tej Singhji was Thakur Shardul Singhji's grandson by his third son, Sajjan Singhji.

3 Rani Padmavati Devi hailed from Trilokpur in Himachal Pradesh's Kangra district.

4 Princess Nalini Shah was the daughter of Nepal's former ruler, King Tribhuvan Bir Bikram Shah. Together, the princess and Shivratan Singh Deo were blessed with five children, Princess Hemlata Raje (the present Maharani of Marwar who married H.H. Maharaja Gaj Singhji II), Raja Raman Deo Singhji (the incumbent head of Poonch), Princess Rajni Chand (raised by the queen mothers in Nepal and married in Nepal), Rajkumar Ratish Deo Singh (married Renu Singh) and Princess Urmila Raje (the present Rajmata of Charkhari who married late Maharaja Jayant Singh Ju Deo).

Chapter 19: Raja Gajendra Singhji and Rani Priti Kumari

1 Majisab Rajendra Kumari was one of eight children born to Maharaja Mahipal Singhji of Sarila. She enjoyed a privileged childhood between Sarila and Mussoorie.